Struggle for Freedom

Struggle for Freedom

The History of Black Americans

DANIEL S. DAVIS

With an introduction by Vernon E. Jordan, Jr.

Illustrated with photographs

HARCOURT BRACE JOVANOVICH, INC.

NEW YORK

The Claude McKay poem "If We Must Die" that appears on
pages 202–203 is reprinted with the kind permission of
Twayne Publishers, Inc., from *The Selected Poems of
Claude McKay,* copyright 1953 by Bookman Associates.

To the memory of
Whitney M. Young, Jr.

Contents

Introduction

Hundreds of years have not dimmed the memories of oppression; time has not stilled the tears of bitterness, nor has it healed the scars of racism. The contemporary struggle for dignity and manhood is echoed by the struggles of the past. Who are we? How did we get where we are? How can we build a better tomorrow? These are all burning questions asked by a newly awakened black community. Before we can peer into the future, we must look back to the past, a past that is streaked with sorrow and hallowed by heroism.

When the black man looks back to the distant shores of slavery and oppression, he does so not to wallow in self-pity, but to seek the causes for his present predicament and to take heart from the successful story of survival. For the story of black Americans is the story of survival in the face of overwhelming odds; the story of a brave people determined to free themselves from the bonds of slavery and oppression. It is a heavy, blood-soaked past, one to shame the American society that committed awesome crimes against humanity and one to instill pride in black strength and black survival.

Introduction

The story of black Americans is also the story of America, seen from a different angle. The realities of violence and cruelty perpetrated against black people challenge the myths of American history. Brave colonists become slaveowners and traders; great presidents become shallow politicians bartering the lives of black people for electoral victories; proud wars become ventures in exploitation. Black history is more than the story of black people; it is the true story of America stripped of myth and legend, a story in which the cruelty and violence that have marked our society stand bared to the world.

A great black leader, W. E. B. Du Bois, once said that history had been told in such a way as to "make pleasant reading for Americans." The crime of slavery was glossed over; the exploitation of blacks skipped; the hollowness of claims of "democracy" that excluded blacks ignored.

Now we are in a time of truth. The relations between black and white can no longer be buried under a tissue of lies and deception. It's all out in the open now. What we used to call a race problem or a Southern problem is now seen as an American problem—one whose roots are sunk deep in our history. The present confrontation among those who would change our society and those who would keep the status quo that continues to exploit black people has resulted in much friction, but it has also resulted in a new honesty that is essential for progress. If we are not to repeat the mistakes of the past, if we are not to continue on the path of tears that has led to the present confrontation, this new honesty will be a basis for a new approach to the problems of our society.

As we look into our past, we see how history repeats

itself in new guises and new slogans. We can make the links between the struggles for abolition in the nineteenth century and the struggle for civil rights in the twentieth. We see how black people have debated the issue of integration vs. separation from the very beginnings of the nation, and how the issue has always been resolved by the masses of black Americans opting for full partnership in the rights and responsibilities of our society. In these pages, we also read of the cycle that the nation has gone through in its struggle with its conscience. At times it moved toward reconciliation and justice, and at other times, such as the present, it says to black people: "Thus far, and no farther." But each turn of the cyclical wheel has left black people closer to their goals, and those of us commited to the achievement of full parity with white Americans can take heart from the lessons of the past, which show conclusively that concessions can be torn from an unwilling nation.

This story of the struggle for freedom ends with what we now see as the "old" civil rights movement. The issues of the sixties have changed. In the sixties, the issue was the right to sit on the bus; today the issue is where that bus is going and how much it costs to get there. In the sixties, the issue was the right to eat at the lunch counter; today the issue is the hunger and malnutrition that stalk the land. In the sixties, the issue was fair employment opportunity. Today, that can no longer be separated from the full employment of black people and equal access to every kind and level of employment, up to and including top policy-making jobs. The central civil rights issue of the sixties was the achievement of the constitutional rights of black people. The central civil rights issue of the seventies is the restructuring of America's economic and political power so that black people have their fair share of the rewards, the responsibilities, and the decision-making in every sector of our common society.

We stand on the shoulders of the past, and this book presents an honest, clear picture of the black experience in America. Its pages portray the truth, undistorted by the mythologies of the past or by the myths of those who seek to rewrite the past to fit their own philosophy. It starts with the story of the ancient glories of Africa, and through its pages march the heroes of black liberation—the black masses whose struggle for freedom is told with truth and integrity.

VERNON E. JORDAN, JR.
Executive Director, National Urban League

Struggle for Freedom

1. The African Past

In 1619—one year before the *Mayflower* arrived at Plymouth Rock—a ship flying the Dutch flag nosed her way into the harbor at Jamestown, Virginia. Her captain arranged to barter part of his cargo for badly needed food, and when the vessel headed back into the Atlantic, she left behind twenty black men and women. They were the first black people to live in the colonies that later became the United States of America. But the story of those twenty blacks—and of the twenty-five million black citizens of the United States today—begins in Africa.

In fact, the story of all mankind begins there. Archaeologists have found the earliest known manlike fossils in East Africa, and the earliest tools have been discovered in the highlands of Kenya. It is likely, then, that the first men on earth were black Africans. The first of the world's great powers—the ancient Egyptians—flourished on that continent, too. Of these people the Greek historian Herodotus has written: "They are black and curly-haired," and archaeologists estimate that a third of them were black. Egypt had black kings who created one of the richest cultures the world has known, and its black people were among the men who built the pyramids and who developed a system of manufacturing and agriculture.

The Africa that has most relevance for us, however, is West Africa because its people were the ancestors of those Negroes sold into American slavery. Here great civilizations flourished. Ghana and Mali—names that have been restored by proud, independent countries today—and Songhay were the greatest of them. They were among the most enlightened of the Middle Ages—humane, stable, productive.

Ghana flourished after the eighth century. Its wealth and power came from the gold trade. Essentially, it served as a middleman between the North Africans who wanted gold to trade to Europe and Asia and the black people of the south who mined the gold and exchanged it for salt.

The transactions for gold followed a curious ritual. Ghanese merchants would travel south with loads of salt and manufactured goods. They crossed a river, left their wares on the bank, and then went off. The gold miners soon placed what they considered a fair exchange in gold dust next to the goods. After the miners vanished into the bush, the merchants returned. If they considered the offer fair, they took the gold and left. If not, they withdrew again, hoping the miners would offer more. These transactions were the foundation of an economy that made Ghana and the empires that succeeded it among the richest states in the world. They traded in other goods, too. Ivory, nuts, and slaves flowed northward; salt, copper, clothes, figs, horses, cattle, shells, and beads, southward.

In this day of supersonic jets that can cross the Atlantic Ocean in three hours, it is hard to imagine the grueling journeys of these trading caravans across the dangerous desert. Most took two months or more. Ibn Battuta, an Arab traveler, took this route when he visited the Mali Empire in 1352, many years after Ghana had fallen, but conditions had remained unchanged.

His journey began at Sijilmasa, a market center in the desert, where he took on a four-month supply of food. Then his caravan pushed on to Taghaza, the salt-mining center, where "we passed ten days of discomfort, because the water is bitter and the place is plagued with flies." After loading enough water to cross the remaining desert, they began the most dangerous leg of their journey. "We used to go ahead of the caravan, and when we found a place suitable for pasturage we would graze our beasts. We went on doing this until one of our party was lost in the desert; after that I neither went ahead nor lagged behind. We passed a caravan on the way, and they told us that some of their party had become separated from them. We found one of them dead under a shrub . . . with his clothes on and a whip in his hand."

Upon arriving at another waystation, the caravans dispatched a messenger, called a *takshif,* to get friends in Walata, the nearest town, to travel out with water. The caravan depended on this messenger. "It often happens," writes Ibn Battuta, "that the *takshif* perishes in this desert, with the result that the people of Walata know nothing about the caravan, and all or most of those who are with it perish."

Despite perils, the trade flourished, and Ghana's riches inspired legends throughout medieval North Africa. The state expanded its power throughout the lower desert and taxed all goods coming in or going out. By custom, the emperor owned all gold found in Ghana. One story credits him with possessing a nugget of gold weighing one ton. According to another legend, a king of Ghana owned a thousand horses, each with a halter of silk, carpets for beds, and three attendants.

The Arab traveler El Bakri visited Ghana's capital, Kumbi, in 1067, just before the empire fell, and left a vivid description of the pomp and power of this black kingdom: "The King of Ghana can put two hundred thousand warriors in the field, more than forty thousand being armed with bow and arrow. . . . When he gives an audience to his people, to listen to their complaints and set them to rights, he sits in a pavilion around which stand . . . ten pages holding shields and gold-mounted swords: and on his right hand are the sons of the princes of his empire, splendidly clad and with gold plaited into their hair. The governor of the city is seated on the ground in front of the king, and all around him are his vizirs in the same position. The gate of the chamber is guarded by dogs of an excellent breed, who never leave the king's seat: they wear collars of gold and silver, ornamented with the same metals."

But all its wealth and power could not save Ghana from destruction when the Almoravids, a fanatical Moslem sect, swept down from the north in a *jihad,* or holy war. The war that followed lasted fourteen years, and Ghana was overcome in 1076. After that, writes Ibn Khaldun, the medieval Arab historian, the Almoravids "spread their dominion over the Negroes, devastated their territory and plundered their property. Having submitted them to a poll tax, they imposed on them a tribute, and compelled a great number of them to become Moslems. The authority of the kings of Ghana being destroyed, their neighbors, the Sosso, took their country and reduced its inhabitants to slavery."

Anarchy followed the conquest. But around 1240, Sundiata, king of a small country once subject to Ghana, founded the city of Mali, which means "where the king resides." The city became the heart of a new empire that dominated the rich trade routes of the trans-Saharan caravans. Sundiata's grandson, Mansa Kankan Musa, brought the desert trading cities under Mali's control and consolidated the power of the Mali empire. By 1324, his dominance secure, he could leave for a pilgrimage to Mecca, a pilgrimage whose splendor became the talk of the medieval world. He traveled with an entourage of sixty thousand, including twelve thousand servants and eighty camels, carrying twenty-four thousand pounds of gold. Five hundred slaves marched before the giant caravan, each carrying a staff of pure gold. When Mansa Musa arrived in Cairo, his followers spent gold so lavishly that its price dropped and still had not recovered a dozen years later. His fame spread to Europe, where a Spanish map of the world, made in 1375, showed a picture of Mansa Musa on his throne dressed in royal robes and holding in his hand a large gold nugget. The caption reads: "This Negro lord is called Musa Mali, Lord of the Negroes of Guinea. So abundant is the gold found in his country that he is the richest and most noble king in all the land."

Mansa Musa did more than display his wealth and spend it freely. He established ambassadors and agents in Morocco and Egypt, and he brought back from Mecca distinguished architects and scholars, who made Mali a center of learning. The famous traveler Leo Africanus a century later describes how the sleepy desert town of Timbuktu became a thriving city where "there are numerous judges, doctors, and clerics, all receiving good salaries from the king." Mansa Musa "pays great respect to men of learning," continues Leo. "There is a great demand for books in manuscript imported from Barbary. More profit is made from the book trade than from any other line of business."

Perhaps Mansa Musa's greatest achievement was to bring the region order and peace, for upon them Mali's trade and prosperity depended. When Ibn Battuta made his visit to Mali in 1352, after the great king's death, he found a peaceful, orderly society whose people "are seldom unjust and have a greater abhorrence of injustice than any other people. The sultan shows no mercy to anyone who is guilty of the least act of it."

Like Ghana, Mali, too, was fated to decline. The subject states that it forced to pay tribute grew restive. After 1400 the trading city of Gao rebelled, and the desert tribesmen sacked the northern market cities. With Gao as its center, a new empire, Songhay, arose in West Africa. Its ambitious ruler, Sonni Ali, built a powerful navy, which controlled the Niger River, and his armies marched victoriously into Timbuktu, Jenne, and, finally, into the heartland of the Mali empire itself.

Sonni Ali's successor, Askia Muhammad I, richly deserves the name he is remembered by—Askia the Great. He came to the throne in 1493 and extended Songhay's power from the shores of the Atlantic to the far reaches of the desert and to the forest regions of the south. His administration encouraged education, created an efficient centralized bureaucracy, fostered trade, and brought prosperity to his people. In 1528 Askia the Great, blind and ill, was overthrown, and turmoil followed as the old antagonisms between town and countryside flared again. Askia Dawud, who came to the throne in 1549, restored harmony, but the enormous size of the empire, its lack of natural defense barriers, and the many and conflicting interests of its people left Songhay vulnerable.

Once again, destruction came from the north. In 1590, Songhay's fabulous wealth tempted Morocco, which sent an army across the desert—eight thousand camels, one thousand pack horses, thirty-one thousand pounds of gunpowder, cavalry armed with spears, and infantry armed with small cannon and the most up-to-date guns. The larger Songhay armies were routed by the Moroccan's firepower, and the empire fell. Prosperity never returned to the region. By the time the Moroccans left, in 1618, the trans-desert trade had given way to a growing sea trade on the western coast of Africa. The day of the great West African empires had ended.

Ghana, Mali, and Songhay were the three great empires of West Africa, but other states, too, grew powerful and prosperous. To the east, in central Africa on the shores of Lake Chad, the Kanem-Bornu empire held sway for more than eight hundred years before it fell in the seventeenth century. It was often strong enough to demand allegiance—and tribute—from the peoples of a vast region. At other times, kings of tribes within its territory seized power. Kanem-Bornu was at its strongest at about the same time its neighbor, Songhay, fell to the Moroccans. Under Mai Idris, military instructors were brought from Tripoli to train an army whose chain-mailed, iron-helmeted musketeers held the area in a vicelike grip. But, like other federal states, Kanem-Bornu splintered when its subject peoples revolted.

The Mossi States, located where the present nation of Upper Volta is today, lasted until the French invasion of the nineteenth century. They were a group of cities allied to resist Islam and the armies of the great empires to the north. The Hausa States, in what is now northern Nigeria, also developed a civilization that withstood outside forces.

The world has much to learn from these complex, highly developed African civilizations. Their warfare, for example, was sparing of human life. True, defeated armies often suffered harshly, and many were sometimes enslaved, but there were not the wholesale killings that made medieval European warfare so bloody. The Azanda of central Africa conducted wars on the principle that victory was theirs if they forced the enemy to withdraw; their battle plans always left the enemy an escape route. The Azanda also began most battles in the late afternoon to allow the losing side to flee under cover of darkness. King Shamba Bolongongo, a seventeenth-century ruler of the Bushongo people of the southern Congo, forbade knife-throwing in warfare. And many of the campaigns of the great empires of the Sudan lasted no more than three or four days, after which the vanquished resumed their lives much as before, except that they now owed allegiance and paid tribute to the victors.

This relative mildness extended also to African justice. The Manicongo kingdom (covering parts of the present-day Congo and Angola) often punished crime with exile; but after ten or twelve years the offender was pardoned and treated with respect. Often, he received an administrative post and was honored as one who knew suffering and had repented. The results of their system impressed European travelers. As late as the nineteenth century, Dr. David Livingstone wrote that there was "perfect security for life and property."

The same gentleness pervaded the life of the people. Introductions and chance meetings in public were occasions of extravagant ritual, marking respect for others and their position in society. Children were taught to honor their parents and to respect the elderly. Among some peoples, the young had obligations to their elders that included service and even labor.

In general, African society presented a picture of peace, stability, and civilization. Mungo Park, the famous Scottish explorer who penetrated deep into the continent in the late 1700s, wrote of Segu, on the Niger River: "The view of this extensive city, the numerous canoes upon the river, the crowded population, and the cultivated state of the surrounding country, found altogether a prospect of civilization and magnificence, which I little expected to find in the bosom of Africa."

West Africans rank among the more advanced people of the sixteenth century. They discovered medicinal herbs, cultivated cattle in an unhospitable climate, developed tropical crops, and were skilled in mining, manufacturing, and weaving. The primitive mining methods of the period make their accomplishments even more impressive. West African miners wrested about nine tons of gold from the earth annually. Four hundred years later colonial governments using modern machinery could do no better than twenty-one tons. A Portuguese traveler in what is now the Congo related that its people wove beautiful fabrics. "Some of them closely resemble velvet; others are so richly adorned with various decorations and arabesques that it is a wonder that anyone working with leaves from the palm and other trees could make such fine and beautiful fabrics, which are every bit as good as silk."

Most African states had kings, who, like those in Europe, thought they ruled by divine right. In the Congo, the same words used to describe the power of the king were also used to describe the grandeur of God. But the African political system allowed room for democratic practices. Councils of elders often elected the kings and could also remove them. Among the Yoruba, in what is now Nigeria, the council let the *Alafin* (or king) know that he was being deposed by sending him an ostrich egg.

Almost all states limited the king's power in one form or another. For example, some councils made up of the heads of local families or clans chose provincial governors and village chiefs. And the larger states had a form of civil service. When Islam came to West Africa, its stress on one God and the teachings of the Koran weakened the powers of the clans and the priesthood and increased the power of the king.

The religions of West Africa were similar, although local groups varied in the details of belief, and held that their gods were their own. Unlike Moslems and Christians, they did not try to convert others to their religions. Often, there was a supreme God, the creator of all things, wielder of absolute power. Below him were lesser gods, each with functions and powers, to whom men prayed and performed ritual devotions. Sometimes the lower gods took the form of sacred animals. The Dahomey venerated serpents, and a man who found a pregnant snake on his property would build a shelter for it. Some peoples endowed leopards and other strong animals with religious spirits, which were believed to represent the community. Their religion inspired the extraordinary art of West African peoples, and it found expression in complex dances, songs, and drum music. All of these were paths to reinforce and glorify the life forces.

Ancestor worship was common, and elaborate rituals honored the spirits of the dead. The Bakongo people of central Africa believed their "original" ancestors were among the spirits and forces roaming the world. According to the Bakongo, men who had lived evil lives could not rejoin their ancestors, but became wandering spirits who bewitched the living and scattered bad luck. Like all religions, those of the African people attempted to explain the mysteries of nature, and the many gods and ancestors were intermediaries to the ultimate Being.

Next to religion, the strongest feature of West African life was the clan. These large groups bound by kinship were made up of several generations of adults who traced their descent to a common ancestor. Many societies were matrilineal—recognizing only the mother's ancestors—and inheritance passed from the mother's brothers to her children. Related families traditionally lived together in enclosed compounds consisting of a group of homes and a courtyard. These extended families made up the clans, which were often spread out among many villages. Clan leaders made up the ruling councils, and each clan had special rights and obligations.

Sometimes clans specialized in one form of labor or another, and their influence depended on the value of that labor to the community. Some peoples rotated their kingship among elders of the various clans. A man who left his clan was, as one proverb stated, like "a locust who had lost his wings." He was beyond the security and affection guaranteed within the blood bonds of the clan. In fact, one of the definitions of African slavery was "being without a clan."

Slavery as practiced by Africans before the coming of Europeans was not the brutal bondage it became. The slave lived outside his own clan and was dependent upon a master. Among the Mukongo, a Congo people, the term for the descendants of a slave woman was "children of the house," while children of free mothers were "people of the clan." But this slavery was not perpetual. Among the Ashanti, of present-day Ghana, the fourth generation born of slaves became free and won adoption into their master's clan. Anyone who mentioned their slave background could be sued for libel.

Prisoners of war often became slaves as did habitual criminals or violators of important taboos. Outright sale was common, from tribe to tribe or within the tribe, and on rare occasions, like periodic famines, free men sold themselves or relatives into slavery. But a slave could buy his own freedom, or a member of his own clan might buy it for him, and, in general, he suffered no violence and was treated no differently from other members of his master's clan. In some states, slaves achieved high office, and slaves often became creditors of their masters. Among most peoples, the slave was not a "thing" but a person who was always in the process of becoming a member of the family.

Typical of most West African slavery were the practices of the Ibo of the present-day eastern region of Nigeria. Olaudah Equiano, who was kidnapped as a child and sold into bondage in America, described the very different life of a slave in an Ibo village: "With us, they do no more work than any other members of the community, even their master; their food, clothing and lodging were nearly the same as ours . . . and there was scarce any other difference between them than a superior degree of importance which the head of the family possesses in our state, and that authority which, as such, he exercises over every part of his household. Some of these slaves have even slaves under them as their own property for their own use."

In stark contrast to the power wielded by slaveowners in slavery as it developed in the Americas, most Africans who owned slaves could only mete out light punishments. Serious offenses by a slave were dealt with by a court in a public trial, and masters often could not even sell their slaves without bringing them to trial first. Furthermore, the African economy, a system of limited production and common ownership of the land, worked to prevent the abuses common in America. Slaves were valued, not because masters lived off their labor, but because they enlarged the family and therefore increased its influence.

Slavery wasn't universal—some tribes refused to hold slaves—nor was it always mild. The king of Dahomey killed slaves, sometimes in the thousands, in ritual sacrifices, and the Ashanti were also known to sacrifice slaves. But in most states the worst a slave suffered was a demotion to the bottom of the social scale. Since everyone else was also tied to the village, restrictions on his freedom became relatively unimportant. He could count on being freed eventually or know that his descendants would become members of his master's clan.

A much worse fate awaited millions of Africans— bondage to masters for whom a slave was nothing more than a piece of property, to exploit as his owner saw fit. This was the system practiced by the Arabs of the east and by the Europeans who came to Africa to explore and to trade and stayed to dominate the continent.

2. The Slave Trade

For the first fifteen hundred years of the Christian era, Europeans knew almost nothing of the vast African continent to the south. Of course, they were familiar with the people of North Africa—the Moors still occupied parts of Spain. But they had the most fantastic notions about the sub-Saharan lands where black people lived. Myths abounded of nations of pygmies, six inches high, of cannibals who battered their victims with long tails, and of tribes with lips so large that they used them for sunshades.

In Europe itself, the fifteenth century was a time of superstition, witchcraft, trials, and a terrifying Inquisition. But Europe was on the move. Explorers ventured to Africa, Asia, and the Americas, and a new spirit of adventure gripped the people—a spirit that was to spell doom for Africans. Their civilization was no match for the ships and guns of the technologically advanced European states. African society had solved the problems of government, providing peace and security. Systems of religion, family life, and the arts flourished. This, however, was a civilization of stability, not growth. It produced only what it could consume. There was no surplus and no necessity to invent machines that could produce more. Unlike Europe, it did not develop the educational and scientific outlook that would result in the inventions and discoveries that made the modern world.

Europeans eager to explore Africa were at first stopped by the treacherous winds and ocean currents that kept ships from venturing too far south. Sailors used to sing: "Who sails beyond the Cape Nun shore / Turns back then, or returns no more." When ship design improved, Prince Henry of Portugal, who had a strong interest in exploration, sent expeditions to the African coast. Henry, who was called Henry the Navigator, wanted to trade directly with Africa, cutting out the Arab middlemen. He sought the legendary gold mines that had tempted the Moroccans, and he wanted to find, or to convert, Christian allies to join the Europeans in a war on Islam.

In addition to gold, Portuguese raiders in 1441 presented Prince Henry with ten African prisoners. Three years later a boatload of 235 enslaved Africans was parceled out to the Portuguese nobility and to the church. Soon a regular traffic started, and enslaved Africans worked the land in underpopulated parts of Portugal. The Pope granted the Portuguese a monopoly of trade on the African coast, and by the 1480s they had established themselves as far south as the Congo.

They leased land from local kings and bargained with them for trading rights, and their fortresses soon lined the west coast of Africa. The most famous one was built at Elmina in 1482. There, six hundred soldiers, masons, and carpenters built what was really a warehouse to keep gold and trading goods and a headquarters to make sure that trade was limited to licensed merchants.

By the late 1480s, the Portuguese seamen had rounded the Cape of Good Hope and started up the eastern coast of Africa. Here they found civilization flourishing on the Indian Ocean trade. Arabs, Negroes, and some Indians lived in harmony, speaking and writing Swahili, a language that combined Bantu and Arabic. They lived in substantial cities such as Malindi, in what is today Kenya. A Portuguese visitor writing in 1501 reported that the people there lived in "fair stone houses" and were "great barterers who deal in cloth, gold, ivory, and divers other wares . . . and to their haven, every year, come many ships with cargoes and merchandise."

Until a short time before the Europeans arrived, some of those ships came from China, which sent a fleet manned by more than thirty thousand sailors in 1431. Compared to the Chinese ships with their radically advanced sail design and their compasses, the Portuguese vessels were puny. But the Chinese had turned inward, burning their ships and withdrawing from the outside world. Thus, the way was open for European domination of Africa.

The Portuguese, under Vasco de Gama, were not satisfied merely to trade. They wanted a monopoly of the trade and allegience to their king, and they wanted loot. Ruthless, armed with guns and cannon, they sacked the east coast cities of Kilwa, Brava, and Mombassa. "When the people of Malindi saw them [the Portuguese]," an African document known as the Kilwa Chronicle relates, "they knew they were bringers of war and corruption, and were troubled with very great fear. They gave them all they asked, water, food, firewood, and everything else. And the Franks [the Portuguese] asked for a pilot to guide them to

31

India, and after that back to their own land—God curse it."

The inland empires of central Africa suffered the same fate as the city-states of the east coast. Portuguese soldiers, intent on plunder, destroyed the very trade and wealth that gave those areas their value. Manuel Barreto, explaining to the Portuguese Viceroy the disappointing returns from the region wrote: "There are many reasons to account for the small quantity of gold produced. *First,* the repugnance of the encozes [chiefs], who will allow no digging in their lands, that the Portuguese may not covet them. . . . *Secondly,* the want of population, which is great throughout. . . . But the principal cause of the want of population is the bad conduct of the Portuguese, from whose violence the blacks flee to other lands . . ."

Right behind the soldiers and administrators came the missionaries, who, says one commentator, "very often were only mercenaries of little virtue." With few exceptions, these missionaries were ignorant and arrogant, greedily filling their pockets and behaving in the most scandalous manner. Nevertheless, the missionaries gained some followers. In the Congo, they managed to convert the king, Nzinga Knuwu, who was baptized King John I, and drew up a formal alliance. John's successor, King Afonso, sent his sons to be educated in Portugal. One was ordained into the priesthood and became the bishop of the Congo, the first black bishop until modern times. But even with the Portuguese and the Congo king working together to build a centralized Christian state, Portuguese adventurers and slave traders encouraged local tribes to break away, and the kingdom was reduced to chaos.

What had started as a hunt for gold soon became a hunt for slaves. The Europeans sought not the gold that is mined, but the gold that changed hands when human beings were sold into slavery. At first, small numbers of slaves were imported into the Iberian peninsula. It wasn't until the Spanish explorers opened the New World to colonization that there was a demand for large numbers of Africans to replace the American Indians, dying, as one planter put it, "like fish in a bucket." The food-gathering, hunting, and fishing tribes of the Americas were rebellious, susceptible to the white man's diseases, unused to the hard physical labor that the Spanish mine owners and planters subjected them to.

In 1517, Bartolomé de las Casas, a colonist in Haiti who later became the bishop of Chiapas, in Mexico, begged King Charles V of Spain to spare the last of Haiti's Indians and to import slaves from Africa. It is ironic that the horrors of the American slave system were born from humane concern for the Indians. Las Casas's plea met with success. The king granted one of his court favorites a license, called the *asiento,* to import four thousand blacks into the West Indies. The license was sold later to Genoese merchants who bought at the slave market of Lisbon, and a year later the first ships sailing directly from the West African coast arrived in the Caribbean with their cargo of tears.

The colonists were delighted. They soon found that one African could do the work of four Indians. But Las Casas lived to regret his letter to Charles V. Before his death in 1566, he wrote, "It is as unjust to enslave Negroes as Indians and for the same reasons." Black slavery, however, had come to the Americas, a curse that was to last until 1888, when Brazil emancipated her slaves, the last nation to do so.

The trade in flesh grew quickly. By 1540, ten thousand slaves a year were being swallowed alive into the Spanish colonies. The *asiento* became a ticket to great wealth. Men died for it, countries went to war for it, and the coveted license passed to other nations. The Portuguese could not long hold a monopoly on a trade so rich, and soon other European countries had entered into it.

The English got into slaving almost by accident, when Captain John Hawkins illegally seized slaves on the African coast, then sold them in the West Indies. Queen Elizabeth was indignant at the idea of carrying off Africans without their consent, an act "which would be detestable and call down the vengeance of Heaven upon the undertakers." Yet the profits from Hawkins' voyages proved large enough to risk heavenly vengeance.

By the seventeenth century, the British had their own colonies in the West Indies that needed slave labor, and in order to supply the slave-hungry planters better, the Company of Royal Adventurers was formed. Its list of backers was a who's who of English nobility. There were twenty-seven knights, seven lords, eight earls, three dukes, a countess, and King Charles II himself. A new coin was issued—the guinea, after the name given to the West African coast—to advertise the company. In 1713, the warring English tore the coveted *asiento* from France and became the leading slave trader in the world.

British slavery was based on the insatiable European hunger for sugar. In Barbados and the other English islands in the West Indies, sugar rapidly replaced other crops. Introduced in 1641, within twenty years it dominated the economy. Small farmers were forced out to make room for huge sugar plantations. In 1645, fewer than one in four Barbadans was a slave, but only twenty years later, whites were a small minority surrounded by an enslaved black population.

The West Indies were the center for what became known as the Triangular Trade. English goods—textiles, metals, manufactured articles, and liquor—were exchanged for slaves on the African coast. The slaves were shipped across the Atlantic in a dreaded trip called the "Middle Passage" and sold in the West Indies. Sugar was bought with the proceeds, and the triangle was completed by ships carrying the sugar to England.

By the eighteenth century, the North American colonies had developed their own Triangular Trade. New England vessels carried rum to the African coast, to be exchanged for slaves, who were sold in the West Indies. The New Englanders invested their earnings in West Indian molasses, which they transported home to convert into more rum, some of which went to buy still more slaves. In 1750, Massachusetts alone had sixty-three distilleries, and the rum trade supported much of New England, giving the ladies of its first families the wealth to dress in finery, and the men the leisure to talk about freedom and liberty.

The Dutch dominated the slave trade for a period in the seventeenth century. They seized the Portuguese fort at Elmina, and even held part of Brazil and other colonies. It was partly to avoid depending upon the Dutch for their slaves that the English and French entered the trade by forming national companies. The economic theory of the period held that a nation's wealth, and therefore its power, depended on how much gold and silver it held. Rather than give their gold and silver to the Dutch for slaves needed by the colonies, the other powers outfitted their own ships and backed adventurers who sailed to the African coast.

The rivalry was intense. Slaves were taken from all along the three-thousand-mile coast—from Senegal to the Congo—but most came from the Slave Coast, along what is now Dahomey, Togo, and Nigeria. Here the Portuguese, English, Dutch, Germans, Swedes, and Danes constructed forts and wooed the coastal monarchs. Wars erupted between traders and soldiers from the monopoly companies. Cape Coast Castle, the strongest fort on the coast after Elmina, changed hands five times within twelve years. Finally, when ruin threatened the trade, the powers agreed on peaceful competition. The national companies bit off regions of the African coast, without consulting the Africans, but could not preserve these as monopolies even among themselves. Independent traders poached on company territory, scorning threats of capital punishment.

The success of the trade depended upon the willing cooperation of the coastal kings. The African genius for organization and for statecraft, which brought the empires of West Africa to a high level of civilization, now employed itself in dooming many millions of Africans to lives of slavery. Only a sophisticated political and commercial system could have insured delivery of over a hundred thousand people a year to the European traders. Ottobah Cugoano, a slave who was later freed and who published his autobiography, fully recognized that the trade in flesh involved black merchants as well as black merchandise. "I must

36

own, to the shame of my own countrymen," he wrote, "that I was first kidnapped and betrayed by my own complexion, who were the first cause of my exile and slavery; but, if there were no buyers, there would be no sellers."

The Europeans vied for favor. They entertained the African kings lavishly, gave them handsome gifts, and even took some of them to Europe. The kings, for their part, were masterly in playing the traders off against one another, driving good bargains for human cargoes while holding on to their powers. They made the Europeans pay rent for their forts, insisted on complete control of trade with the inland states, and charged fees for the right to trade. As a seventeenth-century Dutch report put it: "Nobody is allowed to buy anything from Europeans on the coast except the agents and merchants whom the king has named for this purpose. As soon as one of our ships drops anchor, the people inform the king, and the king appoints two or three agents and twenty or thirty merchants whom he empowers to deal with the Europeans." And the trader John Barbot reported: "Europeans usually give the king the value of fifty slaves in goods, for his permission to carry on the trade, as well as paying customs duties in respect of each ship. They also give the king's son the value of two slaves for the privilege of obtaining water for their crews, and the value of four slaves for permission to cut timber."

Not all monarchs were willing to fatten on the flesh of their countrymen. In 1526, Afonso, king of the Bakongo, wrote the king of Portugal that traders were "grabbing and selling" his people, and asked him, in vain, to call the slavers off because "it is our will that in these kingdoms of the Congo there should not be any trade in slaves." The Al-

37

mamy (ruler) of Futa Toro in what is now northern Senegal decreed that no slaves would be allowed to pass through his lands, and he returned the presents with which French slavers tried to bribe him. But other routes were arranged, and the French had only to move farther down the coast to get their slaves.

The temptations were just too great. The kings wanted the luxuries the Europeans brought. They wanted the fast imported horses, the fancy woolens, the swords, the medicines, the elaborate jewelry, the rum—and the guns. Above all, they needed the guns. With guns, they could beat back stronger states. With guns, they could make lightning raids for slaves inland. With guns, they could capture still more slaves in warfare, trading them for the luxury items in the holds of the slave ships. Without guns, they themselves became the hunted, future slaves for the sugar plantations of the West Indies.

The Europeans wanted slaves, and if guns were the price, they would pay it. But William Bosman, a Dutch trader, expressed their uneasiness about selling guns. "In doing this," he wrote, "we offer them a knife with which to cut our own throats. But we were forced to do this. For if we did not do it, they would easily get enough muskets from the English or from the Danes or from the Prussians. And even if we governors could all agree to stop selling firearms, the private traders of the English or the Dutch would still go on selling them." So the gunsmiths of Birmingham, England, kept their furnaces blazing; at the height of the trade in the eighteenth century, they sent a hundred thousand rifles to the coast in a year.

Wars among the African kingdoms were by this time

the prime means of getting slaves for sale. No longer were they simply waged in self-defense or to settle affairs of honor, and the traditional warfare of the kingdoms, limited by strategy or religious scruples, disappeared. War was now a means of capturing slaves for sale, and the side that seized the largest number of prisoners was the victor. Peaceful agricultural states were transformed into war machines with but one purpose—to sell their brothers into slavery.

The coastal kings often bought slaves from their inland neighbors, sometimes with goods sent on credit by the Europeans. The captives were brought to the coast by overland routes in coffles, or chain gangs. Ropes or leather tongs tied around their necks, the noose of each slave tied to the next, they were marched, sometimes hundreds of miles, to the shore.

When the supply of slaves was low and European ships were waiting with empty holds offshore, the kings formed raiding parties of as many as three thousand soldiers, to attack and set fire to villages and seize prisoners. Sometimes trading and raiding were combined. An English sailor who went along on one of these expeditions reported: "In the daytime we called at the villages as we passed and purchased our slaves fairly; but in the night we made several excursions on the banks of the river. The canoes were usually left with an armed force; the rest, when landed, broke into the villages, and, rushing into the huts of the inhabitants, seized men, women, and children . . ."

Occasionally the tables were turned, and the sellers became the bought. The story was told of one African who threw himself into the kidnapping business with gusto, supplying hundreds of slaves to the Europeans. One day he was captured himself. Like chattel, he was offered to one of his own best customers. "You won't buy me, whom you know to be a great trading man, will you, Captain?" "If they will sell you I will buy you, be you what you may," came the answer. And so he was Indies-bound.

Other black men came aboard ship to sell slaves or to trade and were simply locked in the hold. Such practices would bring the trade to a standstill, and one English captain explained to the Royal Africa Company, "As for trade, I have met with very little, the blacks being afraid to come aboard English ships, they having been tricked by several." Other forms of trickery abounded, and the Africans soon became acquainted with the various methods the Europeans used to cheat them. Experience taught them that they'd be shortchanged and receive less goods than they'd bargained for.

For the most part, though, the trade forced Europeans to deal fairly and to respect local customs. A Dutchman in Benin, now a part of Nigeria, found the people there "good-natured and very civil," but cautioned that "they certainly expect that their good manners shall be repaid in the same way, and not with arrogance and rudeness. . . . They are very prompt in business, and they will not allow any of their ancient customs to be set aside. But once we comply with these customs, then the people of Benin are very easy to deal with, and will leave out nothing needed for a good agreement . . ."

"Good agreements," however, meant brutal slavery for the captives in the factories—slavepens circled by thorn-filled moats and sharp-pointed log fences. Here the river canoes and overland coffles emptied their loads of prisoners and kidnap victims, to await the slave ships—human merchandise, under the eyes of armed guards, ready for shipment. "Though some of them sustained the hardships of their situation with amazing fortitude," reported the explorer Mungo Park, "the greater part were very dejected, and would sit all day in a sort of sullen melancholy, with their eyes fixed upon the ground."

To the pain of leaving family and friends, the horrors of capture and imprisonment, and fears for their future in slavery were added the gross indignities of the initial sale and "inspection." These were conducted in an open area where the captives were stripped naked and subjected to inspection by doctors, who forced them to jump and stretch to test their stamina, and to show their teeth, as a means of estimating age. At the conclusion of the physical examination, sailors took steaming hot irons bearing the letter of the ship's name and branded the helpless, screaming slaves on the breast or shoulder. The slaves were then returned to their pens, fed on bread and water, and left to wait until the Europeans and the merchants and monarchs of the coast had collected enough men and women to fill the holds of the death ships waiting in the harbor.

3. The Hell Ships

From the moment the slaves boarded the vessels, naked and chained, the voyage across the ocean was a foretaste of hell. Olaudah Equiano describes his experience: "When I looked round the ship and saw a large furnace of copper boiling and a multitude of black people of every description chained together, every one of their countenances expressing dejection and sorrow, I no longer doubted my fate; and quite overpowered with horror and anguish, I fell motionless on the deck and fainted. When I recovered I found some black people about me. I asked them if we were not to be eaten by those white men with horrible looks, red faces, and loose hair."

The ocean voyage took anywhere from three weeks to three months, depending on the destination, the course, and the winds. For all this time the slaves were confined in the hold. Most holds were about five feet high, with a built-in platform dividing the space into two horizontal layers. Some were six feet high, but the extra twelve inches were used for yet another platform, so that each person had only twenty inches of headroom, just about enough space for a full-grown man lying on his back to bend his knees.

Within this area, wrote John Newton, a slave-ship captain, the slaves were made to lie "close to each other like books upon a shelf. I have known them so close that the shelf would not easily contain one more. The poor creatures, thus cramped, are likewise in irons for the most part which makes it difficult for them to turn or move or attempt to rise or lie down without hurting themselves or each other. Every morning, perhaps, more instances than one are found of the living and the dead fastened together." Another observer noted: "Each slave had less room than a man in a coffin." Some ship captains were "loose packers" and preferred giving the slaves more room so that they had a better chance of surviving. But most were "tight packers," who argued that by filling every last bit of space they could bring over more slaves and realize greater profits.

England finally passed a law in 1788 regulating the number of slaves a vessel could carry. Subsequently, Captain Parrey of the Royal Navy was sent to measure slaving ships at Liverpool. One typical vessel he inspected, which had a legal limit of 454 slaves, had places for 451 drawn on the ship's diagram. After measuring every inch of the hold, Parrey said he couldn't see how the other three could possibly be squeezed in, but the same ship had carried more than 600 on previous voyages.

The holds were scrubbed down, though the frequency varied with the whims of the ship's captain. "We are very nice in keeping the places where the slaves lie clean and neat," wrote one captain with the self-satisfaction of one who knows his decency is unusual.

Alexander Falconbridge, a ship's doctor, describes going into a hold, which was so "hot as to be sufferable for a very short time. But the excessive heat was not the only thing that rendered their situation intolerable. The deck, that is the floor of their rooms, was so covered with blood and mucous, which had proceeded from them in consequence of the flux, that it resembled a slaughter-house. It is not in the power of the human imagination to picture to itself a situation more dreadful or disgusting. Numbers of the slaves having fainted, they were carried up on deck, where several of them died and the rest were, with great difficulty, restored. It nearly proved fatal to me also." Equiano, who made the voyage as a slave, wrote that "the shrieks of the women and the groans of the dying rendered the whole a scene of horror almost inconceivable."

Small wonder, then, that the ships bound for Rio de Janeiro were known as *tumberios,* the Portuguese word for tomb. Smallpox and dysentery were among the diseases that doomed survivors of the spoiled food and infected water. About one of every seven captives died during the voyage, and one in twenty died shortly after the ship reached its destination.

A sick slave could infect an entire cargo, and captains felt justified in throwing them overboard. Sometimes the real motive was insurance money, for policies did not cover deaths by thirst or sickness. The captain of the *Zong* ordered his crew to jettison 133 slaves for this reason, and an English jury, ruling on the contested insurance claim, said that the "case of the slaves was the same as if horses had been thrown overboard." The verdict was in favor of the *Zong*'s owners, but a higher court reversed the decision.

Some captives preferred suicide to slavery. To counteract their melancholy and to provide at least some exercise, the captives were brought up on deck daily for what was called "dancing the slaves": "Those who were in irons were ordered to stand up and make what motions they could, leaving a passage for such as were out of irons to dance around the deck," wrote Dr. Thomas Trotter, surgeon of the *Brookes.*

The companies took elaborate precautions, not always successful, to prevent slave revolts. Barbot reports that his men visited the holds daily, "narrowly searching every corner between decks, to see whether they have not found means to gather any pieces of iron, or wood, or knives about the ship." On Thomas Phillips' vessel, when the slaves were brought on deck to be fed, sailors were ordered to "stand to their arms, and some with lighted matches at the great guns [cannons]," which they kept loaded and aimed at the slaves.

Even the certainty of barbaric punishment, though, couldn't stop slaves from striking out against their oppressors, and there were hundreds of mutinies aboard slave ships. Dr. Falconbridge wrote: "As very few of the Negroes can so far brook the loss of their liberty, and the hardships they endure, as to bear them with any degree of patience, they are ever upon the watch to take advantage of the least negligence of their oppressors. Insurrections are frequently the consequences; which are seldom suppressed without much bloodshed. Sometimes these are successful, and the whole ship's company is cut off. They are likewise ready to seize every opportunity for committing some act of desperation to free themselves from their miserable state; and notwithstanding the restraints under which they are laid, they often succeed."

At one of the coastal "factories," one captive caught the eye of John Atkins, a ship's surgeon. "I could not help taking notice of one fellow among the rest, of a tall strong Make, and bold, stern aspect." He was called Captain Tomba and had been a leader of a group of inland villages who made a practice of raiding slaving parties and setting slave-trader's huts on fire. Tomba refused to be examined by the slave traders and was whipped unmercifully. Once aboard ship, he led three of his four men in a revolt, with the help of a woman lookout. Armed with hammers, they killed several sailors before they could be overwhelmed. Tomba and another slave, who was also too valuable to be killed, were whipped. But their accomplices were "sentenced to cruel Deaths" by the captain, who made them "first eat the Heart and Liver of one of them killed. The woman he hoisted up by the Thumbs, whipp'd and slashed her with knives, before the other slaves till she died."

Such cruelty came easily to the masters and crews of the slave ships, who were described by a Liverpool slave captain, Hugh Crow, as "the very dregs of the community." Slaving was a dirty business, and crewmen were asked few questions when they signed on a vessel. Many were runaway criminals.

Some of the sailors were themselves kidnapped, for the docks of Liverpool and Bristol were crawling with "crimps," men who tricked sailors aboard the slaving vessels. Once on the ship, the sailors suffered in many of the same ways as the African captives in the hold. Flogging was common. Equiano, who saw a sailor whipped to death, wrote, "I had never seen among my people such instances of brutal cruelty, and this not only shown towards us blacks but also to some of the whites themselves." In fact, sailors died at a higher rate than slaves. They made both legs of the voyage, while slaves made only one. Also, slaves were worth money, while dead sailors couldn't collect wages at the end of a trip and were easily replaced. Truly, as Sir George Young of the Royal Navy told Parliament, the slave trade was "a grave for seamen."

At the height of the slave trade, other ships were also headed for the plantations of the West Indies and the mainland colonies. They were filled with immigrants from Britain and Europe, who took part in the great population movements of the seventeenth and eighteenth centuries. Men and women who had no money but wished to flee the poverty and cruelty of Europe could do so by becoming indentured servants. They received free passage in return for binding themselves to work as servants for a specified time, usually seven to fourteen years.

Agents traveled throughout Europe to recruit emigrants to populate the American colonies, and there were laws that made transportation to the colonies the punishment for such offenses as the "crime" of organizing trade unions. On the ships conditions for these people were not much better than for the slaves. One woman who traveled from Scotland to the West Indies aboard a shipful of indentured servants wrote: "It is hardly possible to believe that human nature could be so depraved as to treat fellow creatures in such a manner for so little gain." But at the end of the voyage sailors could always sign on elsewhere, and immigrants would get land and cash after serving their time. Black Africans could look forward only to slavery, for themselves and their children. For them, the transatlantic voyage was only a prelude to the horrors of chattel slavery.

When the slave ships docked in the ports of the West Indies, the slaves were brought out on deck, where they were examined by planters and merchants. On the following day, the sick and the weakest slaves would usually be picked out, taken to a tavern, and there sold cheap. For the rest, a fixed price was set, and the slaves were penned into an enclosed yard. At a signal, the gates were thrown open and the terrified captives found themselves suddenly surrounded by white men frantically claiming them for their own.

The newly purchased slaves were marched off to do forced labor on plantations. For the first three or four years, they went through a "seasoning process"—getting used to the plantation routine and new tropical diseases. This seasoning killed one out of every three slaves. The planters ruled by terror because they were outnumbered and constantly feared revolt. Slaves found that burning, whipping, hanging, and mutilation were the punishment for even casual offenses.

The slave system corrupted all who took part in it. A slave's life was cheap, and many planters found it profitable to work slaves to death and then buy new ones. One overseer in Jamaica told a visitor, "I have made my employer 20, 30, and 40 more hogsheads per year than my predecessors and tho I have killed 30 to 40 Negroes per year more, yet the produce has been more than adequate to the loss." As a bit of doggerel from the pen of an eighteenth century planter put it:

"I pity them greatly, but I must be mum
    for how could we do without sugar and rum."

It was not just the planters who were corrupted. The citizens of Liverpool, capital of the slave trade, played the slave trade as people in the twentieth century played the stock market. Everyone wanted to buy a piece of a slave ship. An eighteenth-century history of the city says: "Almost every man . . . is a merchant, and he who cannot send a bale will send a bandbox. . . . It is well known that many of the small vessels that import about a hundred slaves are fitted out by attornies, drapers, ropers, grocers, tallow chandlers, barbers, taylors, etc., some have one-eighth, some a sixteenth, and some a thirty-second." The Liverpool town hall was festooned with stone reproductions of Africans and ivory, and shopwindows were filled with handcuffs, leg irons, and other tools of the trade. Goldsmiths advertised, "Silver Locks and Collars for Blacks and Dogs."

At the end of the sixteenth century, Liverpool had been only a sleepy little town, seven streets long. By the 1770s it was a bustling city of 35,000 people, and at the end of the century three of every seven slave ships bound for Africa left from Liverpool's harbor. In the decade 1783 to 1793, ships owned in Liverpool made 900 trips, selling over 300,000 slaves, worth perhaps $400 million in today's money. Profits from these trips were very high, and investors often doubled their money.

Even manufacturing towns that had no direct interest in the trade profited from it by supplying goods for sale or processing raw materials produced by slave labor in the colonies. Woolens from Manchester were shipped on boats from Liverpool; Birmingham gunsmiths, shipbuilders, metal-goods makers, and sugar refiners, all owed their prosperity to the slave trade. In turn, the success of the slave trade was of the greatest importance to England's economy. "It is absolutely necessary," ruled the powerful Board of Trade in 1708, "that a trade so beneficial to the kingdom should be carried on to the greatest advantage. The well supplying of the plantations and colonies with a sufficient number of Negroes at reasonable prices is in our opinion the chief point to be considered."

The huge profits from the trade and from the colonies were reinvested in banks and factories. The blood of slaves was on the money that founded the powerful Barclay's Bank of London, and slavery provided the money that backed James Watt's development of the steam engine. The industrial revolution fed on the profits of slavery. Ironically, though, it was the growth of manufacturing nourished by the industrial revolution that ended the day of the slave trader. Profits greater than any the slavers ever knew were to be won from the new inventions and machines and by tapping the laboring masses of England. Through the late 1700s, the West Indies planters were loosing their dominant position in the British economy.

The new industrial interests in England wanted cheaper imports, while the West Indies planters wanted laws that would continue to protect their trade and keep their prices high. After the American colonies broke away from the mother country, England traded directly with the United States, bypassing the West Indies leg of the transatlantic trade. Instead of declining, trade between the United States and England reached far higher levels than ever before. Free trade was profitable to England's rising commercial and industrial elite, and it was strong enough to withstand the cries for protection from West Indies planters and Liverpool shippers. With the slave trade no longer as important to England's economy and the political power of the planters waning, the stage was set for the country's growing abolitionist movement to win public support. In 1807, Parliament officially ended the British slave trade and with it the era of European dominance in the slave trade.

Europe had prospered from slaving, but Africa suffered. As an English official observed, "From our first settlement on the coast until the abolition of the slave trade in 1807, we did not confer one lasting benefit upon the people." The slave trade ruined African civilization. It plundered the continent of whole generations of farmers, miners, and craftsmen, paying for them with shoddy goods and liquor and undermining the economic foundation of a continent. The race for guns and slaves destroyed the structure of society. The strong and the weak, who once lived side by side in a traditional framework of justice and mutual security, became hunters and hunted.

No one knows how many human beings the slavers stole from African homelands. As many as fifteen million may have arrived in North and South America between the fifteenth and nineteenth centuries. Perhaps another four million died in passage. Adding the numbers killed in slave raids and wars and the victims of the Arab-run trade of East Africa—which continued until a very short time ago—it is possible that slavery has bled Africa of over fifty million human beings since the 1400s.

4. In Colonial America

The twenty black men and women who landed in Jamestown on that hot August day in 1619 were not the first blacks to reach the American mainland. More than a hundred years earlier black men planted crops in Spanish Mexico and explored the vast reaches of the New World.

The first black in the New World was Pedro Alonso Niño, a navigator on the *Niña,* one of Columbus's tiny fleet of ships that discovered America in 1492. Other black men —descendants of Spain's Moorish and African slaves— followed. There were thirty blacks with Balboa when he discovered the Pacific Ocean, and black explorers traveled with Cortez, Coronado, and other Spanish *conquistadores* who charted the wilderness of the Americas. Black slaves outnumbered Spaniards in some of the great outposts of the Spanish empire, like Lima and Mexico City, and they accompanied the Jesuit explorers who planted the French flag in Canada and on the upper Mississippi River.

Perhaps the best known of these almost forgotten black adventurers was Esteban, who led a party of three hundred in search of the legendary cities of gold in the Southwest. He won the friendship of Indians and was able to venture where Spaniards dared not go. Despite warnings, he bravely marched alone to the dread city of Cibola and there, in 1540, met death at the hands of the hostile tribes that guarded it. But by that time he had blazed a trail of discovery through the baked deserts of northern Mexico and parts of the American Southwest as well.

The first black settlers in what was to become the United States were the one hundred slaves who came to South Carolina in 1526 with the Spanish colonists. They were no more willing to endure slavery than blacks would be in later times, and when epidemics weakened their masters, they revolted and fled to nearby Indian tribes.

For the English settlers in Jamestown and other colonies now dotting the Atlantic Coast, slavery was new, but it took root after a few years of experimenting. The colonists knew, of course, about the use of slaves in the West Indies, but the first blacks to settle among them were not treated much differently from the indentured servants. After a given number of years they would receive their freedom, a bit of land, and tools. Some black settlers became masters over others and gave lodging, work, and orders to white servants. But in a very short time, colonists began to treat blacks and whites differently. Gradually, the new rules tightened into the merciless vice that was American slavery.

By the 1630s there were signs that blacks were considered a race apart. A white Virginian named Hugh Davis was ordered to be "soundly whipped" in 1630 for "defiling his body in lying with a Negro." Ten years later a black man named John Punch and two white servants ran away from their place of indenture. When they were caught, four years were added to the periods of service for the whites, but Punch was made a servant for life. Another 1640 case indicates that some blacks were already slaves for life: six white runaways were sentenced to longer service, but their black companion was not—presumably because there was no way to lengthen a life term. Lifetime service by blacks grew so common that in 1661 a Virginia law treating runaways spoke of slaves who were "incapable of making satisfaction by addition of time." Estate records of the period show that blacks were carried on the books at a far higher value than white servants, indicating that they were bound for longer terms, probably for life.

For blacks slavery became hereditary as early as 1646. In that year two blacks were sold to Stephen Charlton "to the use of him and his heyers [heirs], etc. forever." In 1652 a black girl became the property of her purchaser and his heirs "forever with all her increase both male and female." By mid-century then, whites no longer considered blacks men and women; they were goods to be bought and sold.

More and more laws followed, refining and regulating what was soon to be common practice. A Maryland law of 1663 officially condemned black servants to lifelong slavery, and four years later the Virginia Assembly made it legal to enslave Christians. This meant it was impossible for blacks to escape slavery by religious conversion. Other laws barred blacks from bearing arms, from public rights, and from marriage with whites. The barrier between the races grew higher and higher, every crack cemented by customs and laws.

Farther north, slavery came to New England in 1638. In that year, the ship *Desire* sailed into Salem harbor with a cargo of West Indian slaves who were exchanged for Pequod captives taken in Indian wars. Fearing what might happen if they made slaves of the Indians, the Puritans preferred to import Negro slaves. Within six years, when Boston ship-owners began trading directly with Africa, New England had committed itself to the American slave system. In 1641, Massachusetts legalized slavery, and a 1671 law turned the children of slaves into slaves as well.

The God-fearing Puritans wove a web of Biblical jus-tifications for their slaveholding. They thought of them-selves as the Elect of God, with a divine mission to Chris-tianize the "heathens." New England slavery, however, owed less to concern for the souls of black men than to a severe labor shortage. As Emanuel Downing wrote to his brother-in-law, Governor John Winthrop, in 1645, the Mas-sachusetts Bay Colony would not prosper "until we get . . . a stock of slaves sufficient to do all our business." Twenty black slaves, he calculated, could be kept as cheaply as one white servant.

Slavery also flourished in the middle colonies. The Dutch introduced slaves into New Netherland before 1628, and a steady supply of slaves arrived from Angola and Bra-zil to work the rich farms of the Hudson Valley. In fact, only Georgia of all the American colonies resisted the insti-tution.

Georgians made slavery illegal in 1735, mostly be-cause they were afraid that the Spanish in Florida would stir up slave revolts. Georgia's founders also had a vision of a society of hard-working citizen farmers. But the idea of having other men—black men—to do their work for them was hard to resist, and a wave of petitions to the colony's trustees asked that slaves be admitted. One such petition in 1738 bore the marks of eighteen illiterates, who seemed to feel it was more important to get slaves than to learn to read and write. Again and again, the colonists said that white laborers were too costly, and only slave labor could till the soil and make the colony prosperous. They told Georgia's founder, James E. Oglethorpe, "Negroes are as essentially necessary to the cultivation of Georgia as axes, hoes, or any other utensils of agriculture." Finally the pressures grew so great and illegal slavery so widespread that the colony legalized it in 1750.

Colonial America was growing fast. There were woods to level, farms to till, ships to sail. This spacious nation with its seemingly endless wilderness waiting to be settled promised a new start for the surplus populations of cramped Europe, and New England shipowners, southern planters, and others seized their fortunes through slavery. The growth of America very quickly became bound up with the growth of the slave trade and the labor of black bondsmen.

The institution of black slavery, however, provided more than just free labor; it was designed to keep blacks down, to keep America a "white man's country." Others might have been enslaved. The English colonists hated the Irish, and Irish indentured servants frequently served the longest terms. In fact, they were often referred to as "slaves." Indians were plentiful, although it was dangerous to provoke them to war. But only blacks were singled out for perpetual servitude. To understand why this was so, we have to look into the beliefs and the warped imaginations of seventeenth- and eighteenth-century man.

Europeans had often enslaved non-Christians, and black men were "heathens" in the eyes of Englishmen. But in addition, nearly everything else about blacks was different. Their color, their hair, their bone structure, their language, their customs—all offered the European a picture of almost insurmountable difference, leading many to question whether the black was even a man.

A popular belief at the time was that all creatures occupied a fixed place in the Great Chain of Being, with man placed just below angels and the animals of the earth ranked beneath man. Since white men devised the theory, white men were ranked highest. When explorers brought evidence of black men in Africa, they were given a place in the chain below white men and ahead of, though linked to, apes and monkeys. The discovery of black men coincided with the discovery of the manlike chimpanzees, and in the imaginations of the Europeans the two became connected. Medieval European bestiaries, or books of animal lore, were full of fantastic creatures that looked like men. The lurid woodcuts in these books gripped the imagination of sixteenth-century man and made the connection plausible. The association with beasts was persistent. An advertisement for a runaway slave in South Carolina in 1734 referred to him as a "stately *Baboon*" who "has learned to walk very erect on his two Hind-Legs." And blacks were endowed in the fevered imaginations of their oppressors with beast-like sexual appetites.

In addition, the language itself prepared the ground for revulsion against black men. "Black" stood for dirt, evil, danger. Black was associated with the terrors of the night, the unknown, and the workings of the devil. It would be hard to exaggerate the shock the fair-skinned Europeans felt when they confronted men whose skins were so much darker than their own and whose customs seemed so strange. Black men were said to be descendants of Ham, son of Noah, and under a Biblical curse to be slaves forever. A colonial observer noted that "children from the first dawn of reason" were taught to "consider people with a black skin on a footing with domestic animals, form'd to serve and obey."

It was not just the mistaken thinking of the day that led whites to regard black men as a separate and inferior race. The colonists needed cheap labor to raise the sugar and the rice, and so they convinced themselves that blacks were racially suited to labor in places where white men could not survive. They seized whatever beliefs that were at hand to justify the crime of enslavement. Those who bought and sold other men as if they were horses, who drove men in the field until they died of exhaustion, had to deny the humanity of their victims if they were to preserve their own humanity. So the slaughtered slaves became "poor devils" and "poor creatures" and, finally, inferior beings.

St. John de Crevecoeur, a French settler who traveled in the South, described how slaveholders tuned out their feelings: "Their ears by habit are deaf, their hearts are hardened; they neither see, hear nor feel for the woes of their poor slaves, from whose labor their wealth proceeds. Here the horrors of slavery, the hardship of incessant toils, are unseen; and no one thinks with compassion of those showers of sweat and tears which from the bodies of Africans daily drop, and moisten the ground they till. . . . The chosen race eat, drink, and live happy, while the unfortunate one grubs up the ground, raises indigo, or husks the rice."

Nearly all the colonies had slave codes, systems of laws, to regulate the conduct of slaves. These were often patterned after the harsh laws of the West Indies and had two main purposes. They created a legal basis for the separation and debasement of black people, and they established a reign of terror over slaves to prevent them from rebelling.

South Carolina's code, passed in 1712, was typical. Its preface declared that blacks had "barbarous, wild, savage natures" and that laws were needed to "restrain the disorders, rapines and inhumanity, to which they are naturally prone and inclined." The code required slaves to carry a pass whenever they left the plantation. Any white person meeting a black who would not show his pass or who might be a runaway had the right to "beat, maim, or assault" him. Masters were to search the slave quarters once every two weeks for weapons and fugitives, and to keep guns where slaves could not get at them. For blacks, there were long lists of crimes and punishments—whipping, branding, and even death—and measures to prevent slave insurrections. The code provided for patrols, to keep blacks from coming together in groups and from entering the city of Charleston on Sundays except for urgent business. A revision of the state's slave code in 1740 declared "that every Negro, Indian, mulatto and mustezo is a slave, unless the contrary can be made to appear."

Other colonies were equally harsh. Louisiana's code handed whites complete control over their slaves. "The

Master," it stated, "may sell him, dispose of his person, his industry, and his labor: he can do nothing, possess nothing, nor acquire anything but what must belong to his master." Virginia in 1723 even forbade owners to free their slaves except in unusual cases, and Georgia's 1755 code made it illegal for slaves to own canoes or horses, and to learn to read and write. In a burst of kindness, the Georgia code stated that no slave was to work more than sixteen hours a day, which meant that owners were forcing them to work even longer.

Besides the slave codes, there were other forms of control. Even religion was pressed into the service of the slave system. Although whites generally denied their slaves formal religious instruction, since that would make them brothers in spirit with their masters, they often provided a perverted form of indoctrination. Cotton Mather, the famous Puritan divine, published rules for religious instruction of blacks in 1693. Christian teachers were to stress obedience to their master's wishes and promise slaves that if they were "faithful and honest servants," they could look forward to being the "companions of angels in the glories of a Paradise."

Thomas Bacon, a Maryland clergyman, was more direct. In a 1743 sermon to Maryland slaves he said that transgressions against their masters were "faults done against GOD himself, who hath set your masters and mistresses over you, in his own stead, and expects that you will do for them just as you would do for Him." Bacon called the slaveowners "GOD'S overseers" and promised that those who "are faulty towards them, GOD himself will punish . . . in the next world." He told his captive audience:

"You are *to serve your masters with cheerfulness, reverence, and humility.*"

Yet neither the indoctrination nor the harsh punishments of the slave codes could keep black men from striking out against their oppressors. Fear of slave rebellions was constant in all sections of the country, and as the black population grew, this fear came to dominate the master class. By the mid-1700s there were almost as many blacks as whites in Virginia, and in South Carolina blacks outnumbered whites by more than two to one.

The masters had reason to be afraid. The first reported slave conspiracy in English America occurred in Virginia in 1663, and plantations were rife with reports of plots after that. In 1730 Virginia was alarmed by the discovery that while their masters were at church, two hundred slaves had gathered to choose officers and to plan a revolt. Four were executed and many others whipped and imprisoned, and thereafter white Christians went to church bristling with sidearms.

In 1739, a slave named Cato led a revolt in the Charleston area. Marching through the countryside with drums beating and flags flying, he and his followers killed thirty whites, sparing those who had been kind to their slaves. Cato's object was to escape into Spanish Florida, but his band was intercepted and cut to pieces in a running three-day battle. Less than a year afterward, fifty slaves were hanged in Charleston on suspicion of plotting a revolt, and slaves were suspected of setting a fire that swept through the city a little while later.

New York had to call out the militia in 1712 to suppress a slave revolt. Later, in 1741, the city was gripped by hysteria when a white indentured servant, claiming a reward for information about a series of fires, told a wild tale of slave plans to burn the town and kill all the whites. Frenzied violence swept the city and did not end until eighteen slaves and four whites were hanged, thirteen blacks burned alive, and seventy others transported out of the colony.

Fires set by slaves panicked Boston in 1723, and other parts of New England periodically discovered slave plots. Rhode Island, which boasted large plantations in the rich Narragansett Valley, was so fearful of conspiracies that a 1718 law provided that if a slave were caught in the home of a free Negro, both were to be whipped.

Slavery, however, was not so harsh in New England as elsewhere, partly because slave labor was less important to the region's economy. On the eve of the American Revolution, there were only sixteen thousand blacks in all New England. They had rights and privileges denied them in the South: slaves could own property, testify in court, marry in a legal ceremony. In general, they were treated by the law as persons, while in other states they were no more than property. Punishments were far less severe than in the South. A slave found away from his master's house at night might suffer a dozen strokes of the lash in New England; in Virginia, under a 1723 law, he could be dismembered. New England recognized the slave's right to live: a master who killed his slave was, in theory at least, liable to the death penalty. But in the plantation colonies the death of a slave under punishment was not a serious offense.

New England's slaves worked as domestics, mechanics, and sailors and helped in a wide variety of skilled trades. The Yankee's ideal slave was a jack-of-all-trades, who could do anything and fix anything. Except for some Rhode Island and Connecticut plantation areas, the gang labor of other sections was unheard of. In New England, also, black men had better hopes of gaining their freedom. But even in freedom, the laws harassed the black man. He was forced to menial work in place of the military service demanded of other citizens, and he was taxed although he could not vote—but at least he was no longer anyone's property.

Free or slave, black men were set apart from other Americans. Did no one speak for them? Did no one attempt to lift the stone of scorn from their shoulders? Very few. Some religious groups sought better treatment of slaves. The English Anglican Church's Society for the Propagation of the Gospel in Foreign Parts made the most organized effort. For eighty-three years—until 1785—the society's missionaries urged slaveowners to convert their slaves and to teach them to read and write. Sometimes the missionaries founded schools and taught the slaves themselves. Elias Neau, who ran such a school for slaves in New York, was said to have often been seen "creeping into Garrets, cellars and other nauseous places, to exhort and pray by the poor slaves when they are sick." For the most part, though, slaveholders opposed the society's programs, and whatever small help it gave was contradicted by its acceptance of the institution of slavery.

About the only colonists who doubted the morality of slavery were the Quakers, and they came to doubt only after much debate and a long, hard period of soul-searching. George Fox, English founder of the Quakers, pro-

claimed to his American brethern that "Christ died for all
. . . for the tawnies and for the blacks as well as for you
that are called whites." In 1688 the Quaker meeting at
Germantown, Pennsylvania, made the first known protest
against slavery in the colonies. Drawing on the Biblical in-
junction that "we should do to all men like as we will be
done ourselves," the meeting stated that it saw no difference between enslaving black men and enslaving white
men. Then, striking out against the hypocrisy of men who
despised slave traders but owned slaves themselves, the
meeting asked "those who steal or rob men, and those who
buy or purchase them, are they not all alike?"

Despite this plea, Quakers continued to own slaves.
Only a superhuman effort by the persistent Benjamin Lay,
the earnest Anthony Benezet, the saintly John Woolman, and
others converted the Quakers to the antislavery cause. Of
these, Benjamin Lay was the most dramatic. He used atten-
tion-getting devices and civil disobedience methods just as
the civil rights movement more than two centuries later. A
hunchbacked dwarf, Lay once stood outside a Quaker
meeting with his right leg and foot naked in the snow. When
passing friends warned him he would catch cold, he replied:
"Ah, you pretend compassion for me, but you do not feel
for the poor slaves in your fields, who go all winter half-
clad." On another occasion, the flamboyant Lay kidnapped
a neighbor's son. When the search for the boy grew frenzied,
Lay told the distraught father that his son was safe. Now,
he said, the man might understand the feelings of the parents of a black child he had recently bought.

Anthony Benezet established a school for blacks and
propagandized tirelessly in their behalf. John Woolman be-

lieved "slavekeeping to be a practice inconsistent with the Christian Religion," but he became an activist only after a trip to the South, which convinced him that slavery was "a dark gloominess hanging over the Land." He and Benezet haunted Quaker meetings, endlessly fighting over slavery with Friends who professed the Golden Rule. Finally, in 1758, they persuaded the yearly meeting of Quakers to condemn slavery and to ask "such Friends who have any slaves, to set them at Liberty." When the news came to Benjamin Lay on his deathbed, the old fighter said, "I can now die in peace."

However, the Quaker abolitionists were but a small minority, and slavery had sunk deep roots in the colonies. The labor of black men had become too essential to too many people to be dissolved by appeals to conscience. Although ideas of liberty and independence were becoming stronger in the minds of the colonists, it was not liberty for black men that they were concerned about.

5. Revolution and Backlash

England's American colonies grew restive under the heavy-handed policies of the mother country. The colonists resented trade regulations that forced them to sell cheap and buy dear, and they resented the dominance of a king in London, more than three thousand miles away. War clouds were on the horizon as tensions mounted and voices crying for independence were heard.

The first casualty of that war was a runaway slave named Crispus Attucks, a man who knew the value of liberty. In 1750 he had escaped from his master's farm in Massachusetts. He became a sailor and also did odd jobs on the Boston waterfront. Just as much as any white Bostonian, he despised the oppressive British army, sent to keep order in the hostile city.

On a chilly March day in 1770, Crispus Attucks stood among a large group of people that faced a patrol of British soldiers. The crowd was ordered to break up, but it held its ground. When the crowd's taunts grew bolder, the redcoats fixed bayonets and waited for orders. "The way to get rid of these soldiers is to attack the main guard," shouted Attucks, leading the way as the crowd surged forward.

Shots rang out, and Crispus Attucks lay dead in the snow. Four others also died, and that day's events became known as the Boston Massacre. Although the war would not start officially until five years later, Daniel Webster wrote, "From that moment we may date the severance of the British Empire."

At the trial of the British soldiers, the defense attorney, John Adams, scornfully called the crowd a "motley rabble of saucy boys, Negroes, and mulattoes." Historians have followed Adams' view and usually dismiss Crispus Attucks as a tough from the Boston docks who surfaced to take part in a mob action. But Crispus Attucks, as the first martyr of the American Revolution, was as notable in his way as were the slave traders and slaveholders who became the respected leaders of the new country.

When war did come, blacks played key roles in the historic battles for American independence. Blacks were among the Minute Men who were called to arms by Revere's famous ride to fight at Lexington and Concord. They fought beside Ethan Allen's Green Mountain Boys at Fort Ticonderoga. At Bunker Hill, the British commander, Major Pitcairn, yelled triumphantly, "The day is ours," and then fell dead, shot by a black soldier, Peter Salem. Another black soldier at Bunker Hill, Salem Poor, was described as "a brave and gallant soldier" by fourteen of his officers who wrote that he "behaved like an experienced officer, as well as an excellent soldier."

Despite the exploits of blacks in the opening battles of the Revolution, the colonists were reluctant to arm black men. The true nature of the colonists' fellings was revealed in 1776, when they wrote the Declaration of Independence.

Thomas Jefferson submitted a first draft in which he savagely condemned the slave trade, calling it "a cruel war against human nature." But southern planters and New England trading interests combined to cut the passage from the final draft. They left no doubt that they were fighting for the independence and liberty of white men only. Thus, when General George Washington barred blacks from the Continental Army, his order was a reflection of popular sentiment.

The ban on black soldiers, however, finally fell before military necessity. Many colonists remained loyal to the British Crown, and others saw no point in risking their lives. As enlistment rates fell, enthusiasm for arming blacks rose. Alexander Hamilton wrote John Jay, the president of the Continental Congress: "The contempt we have been taught to entertain for the blacks makes us fancy many things that are founded neither in reason nor experience." Certainly, experience contradicted the popular belief that blacks would make poor soldiers, for they had served in integrated fighting units in Indian wars dating back to 1690.

By 1778, most states were enlisting black men who flocked to the ranks wherever they were allowed. Some five thousand fought in the Continental Army. Many took names that expressed their hunger for freedom—Dick Freedom, Pomp Liberty, Peter Freedom were some of General Washington's black soldiers. Other units list: "A Negro Man" or a "Negro." Nameless, forgotten, enslaved, these men fought and died for a dream of liberty. The reality was to be far more distant for them than for their white masters.

For the most part, blacks fought as foot soldiers,

though some served as laborers, some were in the navy, and others were spies. One black spy, remembered simply as Pompey, relayed a secret password to Anthony Wayne's troops that helped them capture Stony Point, New York. Another black man, James Armistead, was a double agent in the service of Lafayette. Black troops came from abroad, too. Among the soldiers France sent to battle the British were 545 blacks from Santo Domingo—among them Henri Christophe, who was to become king of Haiti. Black soldiers were especially important in the Northeast. As one Hessian officer on the New Jersey front wrote: ". . . no regiment is to be seen in which there are not Negroes in abundance, and among them there are able-bodied, strong, and brave fellows."

Although blacks were proving themselves battle-worthy, some states still could not be persuaded to enlist them. When the British threatened the city of Charleston in 1779, the Continental Congress unanimously recommended arming slaves, but South Carolina refused. Washington dispatched an aide, John Laurens, who was from a prominent Carolina family, to raise black soldiers in the region, but he was firmly rebuffed, as was General Nathanael Greene, who also urgently pleaded for slave soldiers.

The British shrewdly tried to use the slaves' longings for liberty to break the back of rebellion. When fighting started in 1775, the British governor of Virginia fled to a warship in Norfolk harbor and promised freedom to all slaves who fought under British colors. His raiding parties struck at unprotected plantations where they captured slaves. Within weeks he had a force of three hundred blacks outfitted in British Army uniforms with the words "Liberty to Slaves" on their breasts. Four years later the British commander-in-chief, General Sir Henry Clinton, offered freedom to any slaves who could escape from their rebel masters to the British lines.

Black men, however, needed no special inducements to escape their bondage: nearly a hundred thousand took advantage of the chaos of war to run away from their masters. Thomas Jefferson estimated that thirty thousand ran away in Virginia alone in 1778. The prominent Virginian Richard Henry Lee wrote that his neighbors lost "every slave they had in the world. . . . This has been the general case of all those who were near the enemy." Three out of four Georgia slaves ran away, many to the swamps of Georgia and South Carolina, where they fought guerrilla actions against slaveowners.

When the British armies left the newly independent states after the peace treaty was signed, they honored their obligation to the slaves who had sought safety behind their lines, taking fourteen thousand with them. Many were settled in Canada. American statesmen bitterly protested, but the English refused to return the freed blacks.

For a new nation, fresh from fighting a war for liberty and freedom, slavery was hard to justify. The ringing words of the Declaration of Independence, "all men are created equal," became ironic in the context of slavery. Many asked, along with Dr. Samuel Johnson: "How is it we hear the loudest yelps for liberty among the drivers of Negroes?" Other Americans agreed with the sentiments of the Connecticut farmer who freed his slave before he joined the army, saying, "I will not fight for liberty and leave a slave at home."

The Founding Fathers were aware of the conflict between slavery and the libertarian doctrines of the Revolution. Washington wrote of slavery that "there is not a man living who wishes more sincerely than I do, to see a plan adopted for the gradual abolition of it." He was determined, he said, never "to possess another slave by purchase," and his will provided for freeing his slaves. In an even stronger statement, the second president, John Adams, wrote, "I have, throughout my whole life, held the practice of slavery in such abhorrence that I have never owned a Negro . . ." Benjamin Franklin in his later years became an abolitionist, and his last public act was to petition the first Congress in 1790 "to contenance the restoration of liberty to those unhappy men, who alone, in this land of freedom are degraded into perpetual bondage."

Thomas Jefferson had deep-rooted doubts about slavery. "The whole commerce between master and slave," he wrote, "is a perpetual exercise of the most boisterous passions, the most unremitting despotism on the one part, and degrading submission on the other." Jefferson feared for the future. "I tremble for my country when I reflect that God is just," he wrote. Nevertheless, Jefferson was a prisoner of prejudice. He wrote that "the blacks . . . are inferior to the whites in the endowments both of mind and body." His belief that blacks could never become equal members of American society led him, like Lincoln in later times, to advocate colonizing blacks abroad. He remained a slaveholder and even fathered a family by a black woman he owned.

One black man of the period, Benjamin Banneker, attempted to change Jefferson's mind. An outstanding mathematician, this remarkable man also designed clocks, wrote almanacs, and was a member of the commission that laid out the new capital city of Washington, D.C. He wrote Jefferson, pointing out that although the Virginian had fought for liberty against the British, he was now "detaining by fraud and violence, so numerous a part of my brethren under groaning captivity and cruel oppression, that you should at the same time be found guilty of that most criminal act, which you professedly detested in others." Pointing to his own accomplishments, Banneker argued that blacks were just as well endowed as whites and deserved their liberty. Jefferson sent him an evasive answer and confided derisively to a friend: "I have a long letter from Banneker which shows him to have a mind of very common stature indeed."

The work of men like Benjamin Banneker was not lost on others and gave evidence that blacks were capable of great achievement when given the opportunity. James Derham, for example, impressed white leaders more open-minded than Jefferson. Derham was a slave to a British army surgeon and absorbed a vast amount of medical knowledge. After the war he was bought by a New Orleans doctor who made him his paid assistant. But, determined to be a free man, Derham purchased his freedom and set up a medical practice in Philadelphia. The most prominent medical man of the period, Dr. Benjamin Rush, met him and was astounded to find that Derham was an expert physician. "I expected to have suggested some new medicines to him, but he suggested many more to me," Rush wrote.

Other blacks made their mark. Phillis Wheatley's literary talents led the Boston family that owned her to grant her her freedom, and she became the most famous woman poet of the period. She was hailed by English critics when she visited London in 1773, and General Washington paid her a special visit during the war. Prince Hall, an army veteran and clergyman, established the first black Masonic Lodge in 1787, receiving his charter directly from England because American Masons refused to give blacks permission to form a lodge. Joshua Bishop and Lemuel Haynes both became pastors to white church congregations.

Even before the war officially began, blacks had banded together to call for their freedom. In New England, particularly, state legislatures were swamped with petitions from blacks that pointed out the discrepancies between the Revolution's ideals and slavery. In 1773 the Massachusetts General Court received a petition from a group of slaves who cried: "We have no property! we have no wives! we have no children! no city! no country!" A year later another group petitioned the governor, saying they were "held in a state of slavery within the bowels of a free and Christian country." In 1779, blacks in New Hampshire asked the state "from what authority they [slave masters] assume to dispose of our lives, freedom, and property," and urged "that the name of slave may not more be heard in a land gloriously contending for the sweets of freedom." In that same year Paul Cuffe, a free black who later became a wealthy shipowner, joined with six others to attack a vulnerable point—taxation without representation, which had been a chief complaint against England. He asked that free blacks go untaxed since they had "no voice or influence in the election of those who tax us."

By 1784, most of the states from Pennsylvania northward had provided for an end to slavery. Some adopted constitutional prohibitions against slavery, some banned slavery through judicial decisions, and some enacted laws that provided for gradual abolition. These laws were not all strong. New York and New Jersey scheduled emancipation, but with a delay of twenty years. What is important is that freedom came to at least one section of the country.

While the libertarian ideas of the Revolution inspired the abolition movement, they were not the only cause. Few northerners held slaves or benefited from slavery, and the competition of slave labor provoked great bitterness among white workers. John Adams believed that this was the major reason slaves were freed. "The common people," he wrote, "would not suffer the labor . . . to be done by slaves. If the gentlemen had been permitted by law to hold slaves, the common white people would have put the slaves to death, and their masters too, perhaps."

Adams may have put it too strongly. But in the South, where slavery was firmly dug in, there was less competition with free workers. There, abolition was out of the question. In Maryland, for example, legislatures voted down bills calling for gradual emancipation time and again. If there were signs of any progress, they were in new laws in Maryland and Virginia against importing slaves and in Virginia's move to make it easier for owners to free slaves. These laws, however, had more to do with a surplus of slaves than with humanitarian ideals.

If anything, the South was more firmly wedded to the slave system than ever. True, the American Revolution had been fought to protect the rights of men. But even more, it had been fought to protect the right to property. For the planters of the South, no property was more valuable than slaves, and their views had prevailed at the Constitutional Convention in 1787. The Constitution barred Congress from making laws that would have any effect on the slave trade until 1808, thus guaranteeing a steady influx of slaves for at least twenty years. Because southern states were fearful of a Congress dominated by the more populous North, their delegates succeeded in including a clause that provided for every black man to be counted as three-fifths of a person in deciding representation in Congress. Furthermore, slaveowners got the assurance that runaways to free states would be returned to them. Protection for slavery became the price of union. Although the Northwest Ordinance of 1787 banned slavery in the territories north of the Ohio River, the young nation bound itself to uphold slavery where it existed.

Southerners were so terrified of their large black population that they fought any changes in the slave system. In 1791, their fears became more acute when slaves rebelled in the French colony of Santo Domingo and eventually took control of the island. Stories of a massacre of Santo Domingo's whites spread from plantation to plantation and panicked many American slaveholders.

In 1793, Thomas Jefferson, then Secretary of State, warned the governor of South Carolina that two black men from Santo Domingo were headed for Charleston to start a slave rebellion there. Several states quickly banned French slaves, and some barred all blacks from the West Indies. Slave plots, real or fancied, were reported in increasing numbers and nearly always were said to have been inspired by the example of Santo Domingo.

In 1800 the worst fears of the slave states were realized. Led by a tall, powerful young man named Gabriel, a thousand slaves armed with homemade weapons gathered outside Richmond. They planned to march on the city and touch off a general uprising throughout Virginia. Perhaps ten thousand slaves throughout the state were waiting for word that the rebellion was under way when nature intervened. As the rebels met in a field six miles outside Richmond, the most severe thunderstorm in memory blasted the area. Roads and bridges were washed out, forcing them to delay their revolt. In the meantime, two slaves turned informer. The militia swiftly captured the leaders of the conspiracy, and at least thirty-five slaves, including Gabriel, were executed.

At their trial, the conspirators showed their determination and their hatred of slavery. One asked that the court execute him immediately, saying: "I know that you have predetermined to shed my blood, why then all this mockery of a trial?" An observer commented with some wonderment: "Of those who have been executed, no one has betrayed his cause. They have uniformly met death with fortitude."

Congressman John Randolph saw the dangers in the spirit of rebellion, which "must deluge the Southern country in blood." The conspirators, he wrote, "manifested a sense of their rights and contempt for danger, and a thirst for revenge which portend the most unhappy consequences." And Virginia's governor James Monroe rightly observed that "while this class of people exists among us we can never count with certainty on its tranquil submission."

Frightened as they were, southerners clung to slavery

and repression. In the decade following the war, record numbers of slaves were imported. By 1790, the year of the first census, there were 697,624 slaves—40 percent more than there had been at the start of the Revolution, despite the fact that nearly 100,000 had run away during the war. Slaves supplied the manpower for the economic spurt that pushed southern production of rice, tobacco, corn, indigo, wheat, and other crops to unprecedented levels.

Cotton was also cultivated, but it was not a very important crop until 1793, when a young New Englander named Eli Whitney invented the cotton gin, a machine that seeded cotton. With more workers free to labor in the cotton fields, production soared. The year before Whitney invented his machine, only six thousand bales of cotton had been harvested. By 1800, twelve times as many bales were being produced annually, and ten years later, almost thirty times as many. At the same time, the Industrial Revolution in England had mechanized the textile industry, and the resulting demand for cotton boosted prices. Planters switched from profitable crops to the most profitable of all—cotton.

Southerners, already importing more slaves than ever, were hungry for even more. In some states, laws against importing slaves were openly ignored, and in 1803, South Carolina reopened the African slave trade, anxious to bring in as many slaves as possible before the Congress could legally end the trade in 1808. There was a mad rush to stock up on newly arrived black men, and planters with "slave-fever" exhausted their credit to buy more and more.

The dawn of the new century saw a hardening of the nation's attitudes toward blacks. Slave codes were tightened and more strictly enforced. Free blacks were special targets.

They were specifically banned from entering Ohio, Kentucky, Maryland, and Delaware, while other states applied the slave codes to them. The ideals of liberty and equality had been forced to yield to economic reality in the South and to open prejudice in the North. Slavery, protected by the American Constitution and buttressed by law and custom, had become far more than an economic system. It was a way of life.

6. In the House of Bondage

Slavery was "perpetual unpaid toil; no marriage, no husband, no wife, no parent, no child; ignorance, brutality, licentiousness; whips, scourges, chains, auctions, jails and separations; an embodiment of all the woes the imagination can conceive." Thus wrote Frederick Douglass, who was born a slave on a Maryland plantation and later became the best-known black leader in America.

There is no doubt that the slave system of the Cotton Kingdom was the most brutal in history. Elsewhere in the Americas, slavery was, at least in the eyes of the law, humane. Spanish and Portuguese colonists were not infected with racial obsessions to the same degree as the English colonists, and the Catholic Church insisted that slaves were men whose souls must be saved and whose spiritual rights must be protected.

In Brazil, for example, the law guaranteed a slave the right to purchase his freedom, as well as some eighty-five days off during the year in which he might work for himself to raise the money. Once freed, he had all the rights and privileges of other free men. Public inspectors checked on the treatment of slaves, and the criminal law made no distinction based on color or slave status. The church provided blacks with religious instruction and with the sacrament of marriage. While southern planters vowed war before they would free their slaves, manumission was an accepted part of Latin American slavery. In 1860, Cuba and Virginia had about the same number of blacks—550,000—but while four out of ten Cuban blacks were free, in Virginia the ratio was only one in ten.

True, the legal rights of Latin American slaves were often abused, and the church's concern for humane treatment probably never had much effect on the rural plantations. On the whole, however, Latin American slavery rarely matched the United States' slave system in brutality.

The main difference between the two systems seemed to lie in their view of the slave. In Latin America, a slave was a man, and slavery a flexible labor system. In the United States he was personal property, in the eyes of the law no different from a horse. As George Fitzhugh, the chief southern proslavery propagandist, put it, "Some were born with saddles on their backs, and others booted and spurred to ride them—and the riding does them good." The slave system was viewed as a positive good, sanctioned by the order of things—the best way of organizing society.

Although only about one of four southerners owned slaves, the whole region was solidly behind the system. Poor whites hoped eventually to own slaves, for this was a status symbol, much as owning an expensive car is today. Those who knew they could never become slaveowners depended on the products of slave labor, worked as overseers, or feared job competition from blacks if slavery ended.

Many people supported slavery because, as an influential journal of the period, *De Bow's Review,* put it: "The humblest white man feels, and the feeling gives him a certain dignity of character, that where there are slaves he is not at the foot of the social ladder, and his own *status* is not the lowest in the community." Similar caste feelings are behind much of the resistance to the black man's demands for equality today.

Slavery was profitable, and its profits helped to create a master class that wielded great power, one whose vision of a slaveocracy became the vision of nearly all southerners, rich and poor alike. Yet, fewer than three thousand families owned a hundred or more slaves. At least twenty slaves were required to farm even a small plantation, but only one out of ten slaveowners held that many.

If there was such a thing as the "typical" slaveowner, he was a small farmer with fewer than five slaves. He often labored alongside them in the fields, and his home was not very much better than the leaky-roofed log cabins of the better-kept plantation slave quarters. Many a southerner has investigated stories of an ancestral "plantation" only to find that it was just such a hovel. But the magnolia-scented myth of a fabled aristocracy dies hard, and the fantasy of a superior civilization in the antebellum South lingers to this day.

The majority of slaveowners had only a few slaves, but a small number of slaveowners, who had large plantations, accounted for the bulk of the slave population. Therefore, the typical owner had very few slaves, but the typical slave worked with more than twenty others on a plantation. Although sugar and rice plantations still thrived, it was King Cotton who ruled the nineteenth-century South, and most slaves labored in the cotton fields.

Slaves worked from "can to can't." Solomon Northup, a free black who was kidnapped and sold into slavery, recalled after he was restored to freedom: "The hands are required to be in the cotton field as soon as it is light in the morning, and, with the exception of ten or fifteen minutes, which is given them at noon to swallow their allowance of cold bacon, they are not permitted to be a moment idle until it is too dark to see, and when the moon is full, they often times labor till the middle of the night. They do not dare to stop even at dinner time, nor return to the quarters, however late it be, until the order to halt is given." When darkness ended labor in the fields, slaves still had work left. "Each one," wrote Northup, "must then attend to his respective chores. One feeds the mules, another the swine— another cuts the wood, and so forth; besides the packing [of cotton] is all done by candlelight. Finally, at a late hour, they reach the quarters, sleepy and overcome with the long day's toil."

Each slave was driven to the limits of his strength. On many plantations it was common to pay special attention to new field hands, who were made to work as quickly as possible. At the end of the day, their load of cotton would be weighed, establishing a standard for that person's capabilities. If he fell below that standard on succeeding nights, it was assumed that he was shirking, and a whipping would follow.

Women had to do field labor, too. Frederick Law Olmsted, a writer who traveled extensively in the South in the 1850s, saw women behind heavy plows. "They were superintended by a male Negro driver, who carried a whip,

which he frequently cracked at them, permitting no daw-
dling or delay." Small wonder that a white Mississippian
told Olmsted: "I'd ruther be dead than be a nigger on one
of those big plantations."

Not all slaves were field hands. Many were domestic
servants—cooks, butlers, coachmen, nurses, and the like.
These had a slightly better life. Their work was easier, and
their food, clothes, and housing were superior to those provided for field slaves. Many identified with the master class
and curried favor with them, looking down on the laboring
hands. But others found that spending the entire work day
under the watchful eyes of their masters was no blessing.
Frederick Douglass was one of these, remarking that he
"had come to prefer the severe labor of the field to the en-
ervating duties of a house-servant."

Other slaves were hired out to nonslaveholders or to
factories. The South's iron industry from its beginnings
used hired slave labor, and the railroads were often built by
black labor, both hired and corporate owned. As one railroad construction project began in Alabama, a newspaper
crowed: "This is the way to build railroads. These eighty-
eight Negroes will probably do more work, and for one-
fourth the cost, than double the number of hired laborers."

By 1860, about half a million slaves lived in towns or
in small villages away from the plantations. Many people in
the cities owned a servant or two, and workmen often purchased a slave assistant. There was very little they did not
do. They were lumberjacks, stevedores, sailors, miners,
teamsters, mechanics, and a few town slaves were given the
privilege of hiring themselves out. Frederick Douglass was
for a time allowed to work in a Baltimore shipyard: "I was

to be allowed all my time; to make all bargains for work; to find my own employment, and to collect my own wages; and, in return for this liberty, I was required, or obliged, to pay . . . three dollars at the end of each week, and to board and clothe myself, and buy my own calking tools."

Such arrangements, however, were rare and usually discouraged because they removed the slave from the master's control and supervision.

In fact, the city itself was considered to be perilous to the system. Many southerners feared its corrupting influence. Slaves worked alongside of workers who received wages, who had rights they did not have, and whose freedom was a constant example to slaves of what life should be. Often, it was found necessary to return slaves to the plantation, lest they become influenced by the temptations of the freedom of city life. Gradually, slavery in the cities declined. In 1820, more than one out of every five town dwellers was a slave, but by 1860, it was one in ten.

Just as many city slaves were skilled workmen, some of the larger plantations also had slave artisans skilled in many crafts. These made shoes and boots, built furniture and farm buildings, wove cloth and tailored fine garments, and, in general, performed much of the skilled work around the plantation. Some slaves were inventors as well. Henry Blair, of Maryland, devised new corn harvesters, and Benjamin Montgomery, whose owner was Jefferson Davis, later to become president of the Confederacy, invented a boat propeller.

Obviously, such artisans were valuable to their owners. So, too, were field hands, especially in the 1850s when prices for slaves reached astronomical heights—$1,000 in

Virginia and more in the Deep South. Many owners, protecting their investment, provided their slaves with decent housing and food, but others were cruel, careless, or stingy.

One Mississippian had twenty-four huts, each no larger than a medium-sized bedroom, for his hundred and fifty slaves. Often, slave cabins lacked windows and had dirt floors. Josiah Henson, a runaway who became an abolitionist leader and was the model for "Uncle Tom" of Harriet Beecher Stowe's explosive novel *Uncle Tom's Cabin,* wrote: "Our beds were collections of straw and old rags, thrown down in the corners and boxed in with boards; a single blanket the only covering." Solomon Northup slept on a foot-wide plank in a windowless log cabin, with the wind and rain sweeping in through the crevices.

Life for slave children was especially hard. Frederick Douglass, according to his own account, had "neither shoes, stockings, jackets, nor trousers." He and other children on his Maryland plantation were issued two rough shirts a year, "and when these were worn out they went naked till the next allowance day," he wrote. They were not given beds: "The children stuck themselves in holes and corners about the quarters, often in the corners of huge chimneys, with their feet in the ashes to keep them warm." They were fed cornmeal mush, which was placed in a trough. "This was set down either on the floor of the kitchen, or out of doors on the ground, and the children were called like so many pigs, and like so many pigs would come, some with oyster-shells, some with pieces of shingles, but none with spoons, and literally devour the mush. He who could eat fastest got most, and he who was strongest got the best place, but few left the trough really satisfied."

Food was often in short supply even for the hard-working field laborers, and they rarely got the nourishing proteins their bodies needed. Although one planter wrote that his slaves were "too well fed," he noted that they stole and killed a hundred of his hogs in a single year. Most plantations had small vegetable gardens, which slaves tended on their days off, but the exhausting work routine, overcrowded quarters, poor food, and inadequate clothing led to much sickness and death. The death rate for slaves was more than 50 percent higher than for whites.

Slavery destroyed not only human life, but also the most basic of all human institutions—the family. Marriage, ruled a North Carolina court, did not exist for slaves, for "it may be dissolved at the pleasure of either party, or by the sale of one or both, depending upon the caprice or necessity of the owners." Some preachers altered the traditional marriage service to read "until death or *distance* do you part." Frequently it was the master who performed the marriage service, sometimes in a ceremony known as "jumping the broom." As one ex-slave recalled, the master would say to the bridegroom: " 'Do you want this girl?' and to the girl, 'Do you want this boy?' Then he would call the Old Mistress to fetch the broom, and Old Master would hold one end and Old Mistress the other and tell the boy and girl to jump this broom, and he would say: 'That's your wife.' "

The black man was persistently degraded and was not allowed to fulfill the role of father and husband. He was always called "boy" and was often described as if he were his wife's possession, for instance, "Mary's Tom." Mother and children were considered a complete family; a slave father was powerless to protect or to control them. A Kentucky court ruled that "the father of a slave is unknown to our law," effectively separating slave fathers from any responsibility for their children. In the eyes of many masters, his role was simply to sire children for his master's use.

A slave woman was a full-time laborer. Her responsibilities as wife and mother were secondary to her master's orders, but countless women overcame all obstacles and, often at the cost of a night's rest, mothered their children. Frederick Douglass recalled that his mother, who lived a dozen miles away, would make "a few hasty visits . . . in the night on foot, after the daily tasks were over, and when she was under the necessity of returning in time to respond to the driver's call to the field in the early morning." One of Booker T. Washington's earliest memories was of his mother "cooking a chicken late at night, and awakening her children for the purpose of feeding them."

Slave women were often forced to come to their masters' beds, a practice one Kentuckian said was "but too common, as we all know." The 1860 census admitted to more than a half million "mulattoes" in the slave states, but this is considered today to be a wildly underestimated figure. One planter told Frederick Law Olmsted: "There is not an old plantation in which the grandchildren of the owner are not whipped in the field by overseers."

Even where masters did respect the marriage bed, the threat of separation hung over the slave family. When Josiah Henson's master died, his slaves were auctioned off. Henson's brothers and sisters were sold to various bidders, and then a man named Riley bought their mother. When young Josiah was put on the block, his mother, Henson recalled, "pushed through the crowd . . . to the spot where Riley was standing. She fell at his feet, and clung to his knees, entreating him in tones that a mother only could command, to buy her *baby* as well as herself, and spare to her one, at least, of her little ones. Will it, can it be believed that this man, thus appealed to, was capable not merely of turning a deaf ear to her supplication, but of disengaging himself from her with such violent blows and kicks, as to reduce her to the necessity of creeping out of his reach . . ."

As cotton exhausted the land in the older slave states, planters moved west, and the white cotton bolls carpeted the new states of Alabama, Louisiana, Mississippi, Tennessee, and later Arkansas and Texas. Slaves were often sold off to the expanding cotton plantations of the Southwest. In the thirty years before the Civil War, Virginia alone exported nearly 300,000 slaves. They were usually sold to traders, who shipped them down the Mississippi River in boats or marched them overland in coffles reminiscent of the African slave trade. Slaveowners in the border and seaboard states kept potential rebels in line by threatening to sell them away from family and friends, to work the notoriously cruel plantations of the Southwest.

There were also other methods of control. Plantation routine was designed to make slaves totally dependent upon their masters and to teach them to obey orders instantly. Strict discipline and fear were the two gods of the Cotton Kingdom, and a black man's life was worthless, weighed against the need to maintain the system of terror. The British consul in Charleston, South Carolina, observed: "It is literally no more to kill a slave than to shoot a dog."

Every hint of insubordination was a threat to the system itself. A North Carolina court admitted that such "insolence" was hard to define: "It may consist in a look, the pointing of a finger, a refusal or neglect to step out of the way when a white person is seen to approach. But each of these acts violates the rules of propriety, and if tolerated, would destroy that subordination upon which our social system rests."

The master's agent in the fields and the man with direct responsibility for controlling slaves was the overseer. Most were poor whites, aflame with hatred for blacks, and they were responsible for much of the brutality. One Mississippian complained that overseers "are as a class a worthless set of vagabonds." Often they were paid by the amount of cotton produced, which gave them all the incentive they needed to work slaves to their limits. One planter told Olmsted, "If they [the overseers] made plenty o' cotton, the owners never asked how many niggers they'd killed." On large plantations, the overseers supervised black assistants, called drivers, who were placed in charge of the work gangs.

Some small farmers became "slave-breakers," men who took their neighbors' rebellious slaves and cruelly broke their spirit. Frederick Douglass was sent to a man named Covey. "It was never too hot, or too cold," Douglass recalled bitterly. "It could never rain, blow, snow or hail too hard for us to work in the field. Work, work, work, was scarcely more the order of the day than of the night. The longest days were too short for him, and the shortest nights were too long for him. I was somewhat unmanageable at the first, but a few months of this discipline tamed me. Mr. Covey succeeded in *breaking* me—in body, soul, and spirit.

My natural elasticity was crushed; my intellect languished; the disposition to read departed; the cheerful spark that lingered about my eye died out; the dark night of slavery closed in upon me, and behold a man transformed to a brute!" The extinction of humanity, independence, and pride was exactly what slave-breakers and overseers aimed for.

Most brutal of all were the slave patrols. These were groups of armed men who regularly checked plantation areas. They searched slave quarters and patrolled the roads on the lookout for slaves who were out without passes. These men were almost always nonslaveholding poor whites who hated masters and slaves equally and took out their feelings on the defenseless blacks they came across. They ruled by the whip, a method of punishment usually reserved for black men. As a Richmond editor cautioned: "No man should ever use a cowhide on a white man. It is a cutting insult never forgiven by the cowhided party, because white human nature revolts at such a degrading chastisement."

Small wonder, then, that many slaves were overcome by fear. Advertisements for runaways sometimes described the man as having an "anxious expression," or said that he "speaks softly and has a downcast look," or "stutters very much when spoken to." But the very fact that slaves ran away at all shows that the spirit was not dead, the longing for liberty not squashed. Much has been written about the submissive character of slaves, but this was often a cloak to hide their true feelings.

Most slaves took every opportunity to sabotoge their master's plans and his property, sometimes by assuming the mask of stupidity. An eighteenth-century English traveler noted, "Let an hundred Men shew him how to hoe, or to drive a Wheelbarrow, he'll still take the one by the Bottom, and the other by the Wheel; and they often die before they can be conquer'd."

Often, hands would slow down, working far below their capacity. They would put rocks and dirt in their cotton baskets to make them weigh what was considered normal for a day's work. When planters experimented with closely supervised picking, production doubled and tripled. Still a watchful eye was not always the answer. Olmsted observed an overseer riding among field hands with a whip in hand, but "as often as he visited one end of the line of operations, the hands at the other end would discontinue their labor, until he turned to ride towards them again."

Even trusted slaves worked against the system. When Solomon Northup became a driver, one of his duties was to punish his fellow slaves. "I learned to handle the whip with marvelous dexterity and precision," he later wrote, "throwing the lash within a hair's breadth of the back, the ear, the nose without, however, touching either of them."

Slaves occasionally struck back at their masters by damaging property. Some planters grew coarser crops because they couldn't depend on slave labor to take proper care of the better varieties, and most farms were forced to use heavy, clumsy tools because lighter ones were broken too often. Mules were common in the South because they could take the punishment slaves handed out far better than horses could. Many a planter grew angry as he compared the well-tended patches of land on which slaves grew food for themselves with his own shabby fields.

Malingering was another sabotage device. Plantation records show that slaves were most likely to fall ill when there was the most work to be done. One slave, believed to be nearly blind, escaped work altogether. After emancipation he miraculously recovered his sight and became one of the best farmers in his county.

Theft and arson plagued all slaveholders. Theft was easily justified. For Frederick Douglass, "it was a question of removal—the taking his meat out of one tub and putting it in another; the ownership of the meat was not affected by the transaction. At first he owned it in the tub, and last he owned it in me." Arson was much feared, for slaves paid back a cruel master by igniting his barns or his harvest.

At times, slaves were driven to more extreme measures. Self-mutilation and even suicide were no strangers to the plantation. But most painful of all, mothers sometimes killed their babies to keep them from a life of slavery. One ex-slave recalled a woman who had three children sold away from her after their first year. When her fourth was born, she said: "I just decided I'm not going to let Old Master sell this baby," and she poisoned the child. Nat Turner, destined to lead the most famous of all slave rebellions, is said to have narrowly escaped death at his mother's hands. To be sure, such occurrences were rare, but some parents preferred to end their children's misery at birth, rather than allow them to endure the living death of slavery.

Runaways were common. Sometimes running away was a means of protest, like going on strike. After excessive cruelty or an increase in the work load, slaves disappeared into the woods, returning when the grievance was removed.

Others ran away to escape sale, to join their families, or to find freedom in the northern states. Slaves from Georgia and the Carolinas often made for Florida, where they became part of the Seminole Indian nation. It took an eight-year war to conquer the Seminoles and their black allies, and General Thomas Jesup declared: "This, you may be assured, is a Negro, not an Indian war." The government finally prevailed in 1842 and shipped the black and red Seminoles to Oklahoma.

The slave system bred desperate men. In several states, runaways formed their own communities deep in the swamps and woods, sallying forth to wage guerrilla warfare against slaveholders. Driven beyond endurance, slaves murdered masters and overseers, or having run away, they killed to escape capture. In 1858, three unarmed runaways fought so desperately that it took fifty South Carolinians to subdue them. Other captured runaways chose death. All these acts unsettled southerners, but it was the organized plots that made their hands clammy with fear. The "Gabriel" rebellion in 1800 was still held up as an example of the power of slaves banding together. In 1822, there was yet another fright for southerners—the Denmark Vesey plot.

Denmark Vesey was a free black, a carpenter in Charleston, South Carolina, who worked for white customers and enjoyed their confidence and respect. He was intelligent and, like other leaders of slave rebellions, a student of the Bible. He paid close attention to the passages that related how the Jews were delivered from Egyptian slavery. His fellow conspirators were all slaves, and they, too, had good reputations. This was what was especially terrifying to the whites of Charleston in that summer of 1822. If the "dependable" slaves conspired to rebel, what owner was safe?

Vesey and his partners recruited hundreds, perhaps thousands, to their planned revolt, but they were betrayed by informers. A round of arrests followed. Authorities had little evidence until one of their prisoners agreed to become a police spy and exposed all the plotters. Some of the convicted prisoners gave more information in order to save their necks, but most followed the advice of Peter Poyas, one of Vesey's top lieutenants, who said, "Die silent as you shall see me do." Thirty-five blacks were hanged, thirty-one more sold out of the state, and four white men were imprisoned for encouraging the conspiracy.

For years the people of Charleston were gripped by the terror of what had almost happened. A prominent citizen, Thomas Pinckney, issued a plea to "reduce the proportion of blacks in the city so that our families shall be safe from the horrors." As time passed, the legend of the plot grew unrecognizable. At least one visitor, retelling the story, declared that Charleston had been set aflame and its white population massacred and that only a last-minute battle stemmed the black tide and won the city back.

Nine years later came the most famous of all slave revolts—the Nat Turner Rebellion. Turner was born in 1800—the year of the Gabriel revolt—and was early marked for distinction because of his high intelligence and extraordinary imagination. He was a religious mystic, who often devoted his time to fasting and prayer. He felt that he had been chosen to strike the death blow to slavery. Searching the heavens for signs, he found his mission early in

1831 when a solar eclipse convinced him that the time had come.

On Sunday, August 21, he and his followers brought destruction to the Virginia countryside. Within twenty-four hours, they killed at least fifty-five whites. Whole families were slaughtered as the rebels marched from farmhouse to farmhouse on their way to the Southhampton County seat. Troops overwhelmed them before they could reach their goal, killing a hundred slaves, but Turner escaped and hid in the woods for two months. Although he was finally captured and promptly executed, the Nat Turner Rebellion left its mark on the South.

Some states called special sessions of their legislatures to strengthen the Black Codes, and everywhere patrols were tightened and masters more wary. Each new report of a slave plot increased the hysteria.

In 1835, a lady in Beattie's Bluff, Mississippi, became frightened at her slaves' arrogance and called for help. The men of the neighborhood decided that an insurrection was planned and formed vigilante groups to terrorize the slaves. The women and children of the area were huddled together in guarded central locations while armed squads patrolled two counties. Before the scare was over, a dozen blacks and five white men had been hanged. One white man, alarmed by the mob hysteria, wrote the governor for assistance, pointing out that the "danger from the slaves vanished at the detection of the conspiracy and another danger has taken place more formidable than that." Nearly all parts of the South experienced similar panic at one time or another. As one planter noted: "It is a disagreeable state of living to be ever suspicious of those with whom we live."

In all, there were two hundred and fifty reported slave plots and rebellions and many hundreds of rebellious acts that fell short of organized conspiracies. Southerners might delude themselves, as one did after the Turner Rebellion, when he said: "Our slave population is not only a happy one, but it is a contented, peaceful and harmless one." But the sleep of the slaveholders was troubled. The club and the lash could not drive freedom from the dreams of their slaves.

7. Between Freedom and Slavery

"A free Negro! Why, the very term seems an absurdity," snorted the southern firebrand George Fitzhugh, and many Americans agreed with him. A South Carolina court declared: "A free African population is a curse to any country." Since slavery was considered the natural condition of black men, the very existence of free blacks threatened the delicate racial balance of society.

Nevertheless, there was a total of 488,000 free black men and women in the United States on the eve of the Civil War, and more than half of them lived in the South. Some had been freed by their owners, who were sometimes also their fathers. State laws, however, discouraged manumission, and each decade saw less of it. Northern blacks had been free since the abolition triumphs of the late eighteenth century, and their ranks were swelled by runaways from the South. But the black man's freedom was relative; he was more free than a slave, less free than a white man. "Thus the Negro is free," observed the brilliant Frenchman Alexis de Tocqueville in 1831, "but he can share neither the rights, nor the pleasures, nor the labor, nor the afflictions, nor the tomb of him whose equal he has been declared to be; and he cannot meet him upon fair terms in life or in death."

Prejudice against blacks approached fanaticism and was often more virulent in the North than in the South. A delegate to the Indiana state constitutional convention spat: "It would be better to kill them off at once, if there is no other way to get rid of them." The vast majority of blacks in the free states were barred from voting, and some states refused to admit them from elsewhere in the country. Illinois voters approved a constitutional provision that banned blacks from entering the state by a two-to-one margin. When a black man brought his fiancée into Indiana, he was found guilty of violating the state's exclusion law. The state Supreme Court ruled: "The policy of the state . . . is to exclude any further ingress of Negroes, and to remove those already among us as speedily as possible."

Often this hatred spilled over into violence. Between 1832 and 1849, there were five anti-black riots in Philadelphia. During one of the worst of these, in 1834, hundreds of black people were forced to flee the city to escape a mob that burned churches and destroyed homes. About the only advice an investigating committee of prominent citizens could offer Philadelphia's blacks was "the necessity . . . of behaving themselves inoffensively and with civility at all times and upon all occasions; taking care, as they pass along the streets, or assemble together, not to be obtrusive." Eight years later in the city of brotherly love another mob fell upon a black parade. State troops finally ended the riot, but not before the African Hall and Presbyterian Church were burned.

Competition for scarce jobs was often behind such

outbursts. In 1834, a mob in Columbia, Pennsylvania, drove blacks into the woods and then burned their homes. One of the grievances was that merchants had hired black men for jobs customarily held by whites. In 1841, Cincinnati whites, angered at the influx of runaway slaves, invaded the black ghetto. City officials disarmed and jailed black men to pacify the mob and promised security for black women and children, but the mob returned "with hellish shouts to attack those helpless and unprotected persons!"

Violence wasn't the only evil blacks had to contend with. They faced segregation everywhere. As an Indiana lawmaker declared, "The tendency, strong and irresistible, of the American mind is finally to accomplish the separation of the two races." Blacks rode in segregated sections of railroads, were often refused seats on horse-cars, and were placed in separate sections of the churches. Frederick Douglass, after his escape to Massachusetts, was once seated in the "Negro section" of a church, where blacks were called to worship only after whites. "The colored members," Douglass angrily recalled, "poor slavish souls, went forward as invited. I went *out* and have never been in that church since."

School segregation was as much a problem in the 1850s as it would be a century later. In nearly every city white children and black children went to separate schools. As an Indiana court ruled, ". . . black children were deemed unfit associates of whites, as school companions." Blacks attended universally inferior schools, starved for funds and trained teachers.

The black Philadelphia abolitionist Robert Purvis refused to pay his school tax as a protest against "the proscription and exclusion of my children from the Public School." Only in Massachusetts were such efforts successful, and when Boston desegregated its schools in 1855, the appearance of black children in the previously all-white classrooms created a sensation, although—in contrast to events a century later—the change was accomplished peacefully. In the South, schools for black children were not segregated; they simply didn't exist. Blacks banded together to form private schools for their children, but these were often harassed by the authorities.

During the War of 1812, some free blacks in the South were given an opportunity to serve in the armed forces. Although most states still feared arming black men, Louisiana, which had had black militia units under the French and the Spanish, had no such qualms. It was there that General Andrew Jackson commanded black volunteers—enlisted with equal pay and equal treatment—in the famous battle of New Orleans in 1815. Jackson paid tribute to the vital role these troops played in the defense of the city by announcing that "the two corps of colored volunteers had . . . not disappointed the hopes that were formed of their courage and perseverance." Blacks were also prominent in the Navy, and one out of ten sailors in the naval campaigns on the Great Lakes was black. Yet it seemed that no matter how willing black people were to prove their loyalty, the white majority was as determined to exclude them from equal partnership in the society.

Free blacks in the South were subjected to strict controls, chiefly because whites feared that their very freedom would endanger slavery. Citizens in Charleston complained: "The superior condition of the free persons of color excited discontent among our slaves, who continually have before their eyes persons of the same color, many of whom they have known in slavery, and with all of whom they associate on terms of equality."

In reality, the line between free black men and slaves was often hard to see. In 1832, the city of Baltimore passed a law making free blacks "liable in every respect to the same treatment and penalty as slaves," and ruled that they would "be guilty of, and convicted of, any offense for which slaves are now punishable." They lived in constant fear of unreasonable punishments or even re-enslavement and were forced to carry certificates proving they were free men, not fugitive slaves. Some states required them to post bonds to insure that they would not become public burdens; others forced them to have white guardians.

Free black men were kept out of skilled trades in some states. Georgia barred them from the printing and construction industries, and South Carolina prohibited them from holding office jobs. In most seaboard states, black sailors were prevented from coming ashore when their ships docked. Other blacks were even displaced from jobs they had traditionally held. In the 1840s an observer noted that "all the draymen [wagon drivers] in New Orleans, a numerous class, and the cabmen were colored. Now they are nearly all white. The servants of the great hotels were formerly of the African, now they are of the European race."

Despite these formidable restrictions, some free black men prospered in the South. Thomy Lafon of New Orleans amassed a half-million-dollar fortune, and Cyprian Ricard owned ninety-one slaves and an estate in Louisiana. In 1830, thirty-six hundred blacks owned slaves; the vast majority were individuals who had purchased their own husbands, wives, or children and were prevented from freeing them by state laws.

Most blacks of the period, however, were engulfed in poverty. About nine out of ten blacks employed in New York were in menial or unskilled jobs, and unemployment was astronomical. Prejudice even kept blacks from emergency tasks. Pennsylvania abolitionists protested that, after a snowstorm that kept thousands of whites working on snow-removal projects, hundreds of blacks were observed "going about the streets with shovels in their hands, looking for work and finding none."

After 1830, the situation worsened as European immigrants flooded the cities, taking even the few jobs available to blacks. Frederick Douglass complained: "Every hour sees us elbowed out of some employment, to make room perhaps for some newly arrived immigrants, whose hunger and color are thought to give them a title to especial favor." The newcomers themselves met with discrimination, and "No Irish Need Apply" signs were prominent in hiring halls. The frantic competition for scarce jobs between blacks and the immigrant groups, especially the Irish who congregated in the major cities, led to friction, street fighting, and even large-scale rioting.

Spokesmen for southern slave interests, smarting under abolitionist attacks, did not ignore the condition of the poor in the North. Senator Robert Hayne of South Carolina gleefully told Congress: ". . . there does not exist on the face of the earth a population so poor, so wretched, so vile, so loathsome, so utterly destitute of all comforts, conveniences, and decencies of life, as those unfortunate blacks of Philadelphia, and New York, and Boston. Liberty has been to them the greatest of calamities, the heaviest of curses." Another southerner insisted: "Go home and emancipate your free Negroes. When you do that, we will listen to you with more patience."

They had a point. Philadelphia's coroner reported in 1848 that many blacks had been "found dead in cold and exposed rooms and garrets, board shanties five and six feet high, and as many feet square." A year later Philadelphia Quakers investigated these squalid living conditions and found that six or eight people often lived in these shanties, so small that a man of slightly more than average height could not lie down or stand up. "An infant, if born in them," they reported, "could scarcely survive there many weeks." These rooms, appropriately called pens, rented for eight and ten cents a night, and the investigators calculated that while a row of them cost about $100 to build, they brought profits of $600 a year, a handsome sum in those days.

Nevertheless, with hard work and perseverance in the face of tremendous obstacles, some blacks in the North, as in the South, achieved economic success. The sailmaker James Forten employed forty workers, both white and black, and he was worth $100,000. Paul Cuffe started out as a sailor on whaling ships and rose to become a prominent shipowner, merchant, and philanthropist. In 1815, he took thirty-eight freedmen to Liberia and became the first black American to organize a society to encourage emigration to Africa.

Some Philadelphia blacks used their experience as cooks, waiters, and butlers to dominate that city's restaurant catering business. Rich white families patronized these establishments throughout the nineteenth century, and no party would be considered fashionable unless it was catered by one of several prominent black restaurateurs. Despite the odds, New York blacks had acquired $2,000,000 in real estate and savings by 1837, and black communities in other cities also amassed some wealth and property.

America's first black college graduate, John Russwurm (Bowdoin College, class of 1826), founded the country's first black newspaper, *Freedom's Journal,* in 1827. "We wish to plead our own cause," stated its first editorial. "Too long have others spoken for us." Two years later Russwurm settled in Africa, where he became Liberia's first Superintendent of Schools. His co-editor, Samuel E. Cornish, continued the paper, now called *Rights of All,* and became a leader in the abolition movement.

Others rose to prominence because of their extraordinary talents. The singer Elizabeth Taylor Greenfield was born a slave, but she captivated opera audiences around the world, earning the title "The Black Swan." One of the greatest actors of the nineteenth century was Ira Aldridge, who became a famous interpreter of Shakespearian roles, honored throughout Europe, although his color barred him from appearing on the American stage.

Some, such as Norbett Rillieux, were inventors. In 1846, he developed a new process for refining sugar that cut production costs in half, doing for sugar what Whitney's gin did for cotton. Jan Matzeliger invented a shoe-lasting machine that revolutionized the industry. Prices were halved and wages were doubled as his machine made mass-produced shoes a reality. Other blacks won prominence through accomplishments in medicine, law, and other fields.

One extraordinary educator was John Chavis, who was sent by a North Carolina gentleman to attend Princeton University as an "experiment," to see whether a black man had the capacity to absorb higher learning. Chavis, like other blacks who had the opportunity, proved his equality, returning to the South with so high a reputation that he established a school for the sons of the aristocracy, even boarding some of them in his own house.

Black men no less than white men helped to open the West. One who achieved fame was Jean Baptiste Point du Sable, a frontier trader who in 1779 established his trading post where Chicago now stands. Other black westerners were cowhands, settlers, missionaries, gold prospectors, miners, trappers, guides, and explorers. George William Bush, for example, led his family and a group of white settlers on a pioneering trip to Washington and Oregon. They were the first American settlers north of the Columbia River, and Bush became a leading figure in the region.

Because they lacked the racial arrogance of white men, blacks were better at dealing with the Indians. Lewis and Clark, for example, depended on their slave, York, a giant of a man who won the friendship of the Indians of the Northwest. An old trapper wrote: "The old fur traders always got a Negro, if possible, to negotiate for them with the Indians, because of their 'pacifying effect.' They could manage better than white men, and with less friction."

Many, like James Beckwourth, settled among the Indians. A contemporary called him "the most famous Indian fighter of this generation." He was a trapper, hunter, fur trader—and Indian chief. He sold the Crow tribe a tall story about being the long-lost kidnapped son of a brave, and he lived for years among them, finally becoming a chief. But he was a restless adventurer, and in the 1840s, he headed west again, to explore mountain country. High in the Rockies he discovered a pass, later named Beckwourth Pass, which became an important gateway to California during the Gold Rush.

The accomplishments of these and other black men and women were impressive, especially when we consider that they faced a stone wall of prejudice at every turn. But their brothers were in the chains of slavery, and among many blacks who enjoyed quasi-freedom were some who saw no chance for a black man to succeed in America. At the same time, many white Americans saw no place for black men in a nation they were determined would be "a white man's country." Calls for sending blacks to a colony in Africa grew more insistent.

The spearhead of the emigration movement was the American Colonization Society, a grabbag of slaveholders and racists, in addition to some well-meaning whites and a few blacks who saw emigration as the only hope for the downtrodden black man. Formally organized in 1816, the society soon commanded the support of many prominent people from all parts of the country, including Henry Clay, Daniel Webster, and James Madison. Some states appropriated money for a black colony, and fourteen state legislatures and several governors endorsed the society's aims. Although fifteen thousand eventually settled in the society's colony of Liberia, most were strongly opposed to the plan.

As the society's director sadly noted, "The free people of color, taken as a community, look on our undertaking with disaffection."

One month after the society was founded, three thousand blacks jammed Philadelphia's Bethel Church to protest. "Whereas our ancestors (not of choice) were the first successful cultivators of the wilds of America," they pointed out, "we their descendants feel ourselves entitled to participate in the blessings of her luxuriant soil, which their blood and sweat manured; and that any measure . . . to banish us from her bosom would not only be cruel, but in direct violation of those principles, which have been the boast of this republic." They resolved not to leave their brothers in chains: ". . . we will never separate ourselves voluntarily from the slave population in this country; they are our bretheren by the ties of consanguinity, of suffering, and of wrong; and we feel there is more virtue in suffering privations with them than fancied advantages for a season."

Controversy over emigration raged right up until the Civil War with support for it coming from those blacks who were so embittered by discrimination that they saw no other hope for the future. They were led by Henry Highland Garnet, James T. Holly, and Martin R. Delany, who argued that blacks might escape American racism in Central America, in Africa, or in the black republic of Haiti. In 1859, Delany was sent by an emigrationist group, the National Emigration Conference, to investigate likely colonization sites in West Africa. Like his fellow emigrationists, Delany was a forerunner of the black nationalists of later periods. Then as now, black people were divided between those who sought an equal place in an integrated society and those who saw no hope for survival except in separate black communities and institutions. Delany was perhaps the most dynamic and articulate of the black leaders who sought to build a black nation on foreign soil. He declared: "Our policy must be Africa for the African race and black men to rule them." Delany's racial pride impressed Frederick Douglass, who said: "I thank God for making me a man simply; but Delany always thanks Him for making him a black man."

For all his influence on black nationalists of a later period, Delany's efforts and those of his fellow would-be colonizers came to nought. The general feeling among blacks that this country was their home, the unhappy experiences of some pioneer emigrants, and the promise of freedom brought by the Civil War delivered the final blows to plans for leaving the country. The militants represented an important element of the black community, but they were still outside the mainstream of black thinking that was resolved to fight for equality in the United States.

Of the organized black groups that led the battle against emigration and were at the forefront of the battle against slavery, the black churches were among the most important. They dated from the post Revolutionary era, when they had arisen in protest against white churches that either excluded blacks or forced them into separate pews. After Richard Allen and Absolom Jones were lifted bodily to their feet while at prayer and ejected from a Philadelphia church, they built their own church, in 1794. Their movement grew, and in 1816 Allen became bishop of the new African Methodist Episcopal Church.

During this period, nearly all cities saw the formation of associations of black people who banded together to help one another in the face of a hostile society. The Masons, founded by Prince Hall during the Revolutionary War, grew in numbers, and in 1843 Peter Ogden and several other blacks founded the Grand United Order of Odd Fellows. Baltimore alone had thirty-five such fraternal associations; Philadelphia and New York had self-improvement groups that encouraged literacy and founded libraries. In Philadelphia Richard Allen and Absolom Jones had organized in the 1790s the Free African Society to provide benefits to widows and orphans and to assist members in need. By mid-century, most cities had similar organizations known as mutual-aid societies.

Despite their own difficult condition, the subject that most concerned blacks and their associations was southern slavery. Many had been slaves themselves. As the abolitionist Theodore Weld wrote in 1834: "Of the almost 3,000 blacks in Cincinnati more than three-fourths of the adults are emancipated slaves, who worked out their own freedom. Besides these, multitudes are toiling to purchase their friends, who are now in slavery."

From 1830 through 1835, blacks held national conventions annually to discuss matters of concern, chiefly the slave system. This Negro Convention Movement, as it came to be called, held periodic meetings in later years, and many states had their own conventions, which met regularly to protest prejudice. In 1853 a Rochester convention formed the National Council of Colored People, which delivered a ringing indictment of racism. In their roles as protesters and in their efforts to help black people overcome the barriers of discrimination, the conventions and the organizations they created were forerunners of today's civil rights groups.

8. Freedom Fighters

Frederick Douglass, who was destined to become the leading black spokesman in America, might have toiled his life away on a Maryland plantation if he had not been sent to live with his master's relatives in Baltimore. There a whole new world opened to him, a world undreamed of in the prison of the plantation, where he had been born a slave. His master's wife took a liking to the boy and started to teach him to read. The lessons ended abruptly when she proudly informed her husband that she was going to teach him to read the Bible. "If he learns to read the Bible," thundered Hugh Auld, "it will forever unfit him to be a slave. He should know nothing but the will of his master, and learn to obey it. . . . Learning will do him no good, but a great deal of harm, making him disconsolate and unhappy. If you teach him how to read, he'll want to know how to write, and this accomplished, he'll be running away with himself."

That is exactly what did happen. "From that moment," wrote Douglass, "I understood the direct pathway from slavery to freedom." Carrying a spelling book in his pocket, he turned to his young white playmates to teach him the rudiments of writing. His thirst for knowledge was unquenchable, and the boy spent many hours hidden in the attic, practicing writing in the school notebooks of his master's son.

When he was twenty years old, he made his break for freedom. Borrowing papers that identified him as a free sailor, young Douglass boarded a train headed north and finally settled in New Bedford, Massachusetts, where he met the realities of northern life. Applying for a job as a caulker in the New Bedford shipyard, the young man was told that every white man would leave the ship in her unfinished condition if he "struck a blow at my trade upon her."

He worked at odd jobs for a while, began reading the abolitionist paper the *Liberator,* and attended antislavery meetings. In 1841, Douglass spoke at one of these meetings and found a new career that would make him one of the most famous men in America. He became a lecturer for the state abolitionist society, talking about his life in slavery. Douglass was not content with merely reciting his experiences, however, and the brilliant young orator expanded his talks to include the social, economic, and philosophical aspects of the slave system.

"People won't believe you ever were a slave, Frederick, if you keep on this way," cautioned one of his white mentors. "Give us the facts, we will take care of the philosophy," remarked another patronizingly. But he was a born leader, not a freak to be placed on display, and he soon became the most prominent black abolitionist.

Douglass was described by a friend as being "like an African prince, conscious of his dignity and power, grand in his proportions, majestic in his wrath, as with keen wit, satire and indignation he portrayed the bitterness of slavery." Over six feet tall and "straight as an arrow," he had a rich, deep voice that captivated thousands as he lectured from one end of the country to the other, thundering at the slave system and demanding equality for black men.

In 1847, Douglass founded the *North Star,* a weekly newspaper, because he felt strongly that black men should play a larger role in the fight against slavery. In the first issue of his paper he wrote: "The man who has suffered the wrong is the man to demand redress—the man STRUCK is the man to CRY OUT—he who has endured the cruel pangs of Slavery is the man to advocate Liberty. We must be our own representatives and advocates—not distinct from, but in connection with, our white friends."

The closest of Douglass's "white friends" was William Lloyd Garrison, a lean, hawk-nosed young fireband who was the driving force behind the northern abolition movement. He propagandized tirelessly for an end to slavery and backed other reform movements as well. In 1831, at twenty-six, Garrison started the *Liberator,* which depended almost totally upon black readers for its support. The *Liberator*'s masthead was emblazoned with the slogan, "NO UNION WITH SLAVEHOLDERS," and Garrison's anger over federal protection for slavery led him to burn a copy of the Constitution publicly one Fourth of July, crying: "So perish all compromises with tyranny! And let all the people say Amen!" Once, during a heated meeting, his friend Samuel May remarked: "Why, you are all on fire." "Brother May," Garrison replied, "I have need to be all on fire, for I have mountains of ice about me to melt."

Their critics called them fanatics, but the abolitionists

needed this kind of zeal, for theirs were almost the only voices crying out in a wilderness of hate and prejudice. Garrison himself had a price on his head. Slaveowners publicly offered $10,000 to anyone who would kidnap him, and the state of Georgia offered $5,000 for his capture. He was paraded through the streets of Boston in 1835 by antiabolitionists and saved from lynching only by the intervention of the mayor, who jailed him for his own protection. Everywhere, abolitionists were attacked, beaten, and sometimes killed. In 1837, in Alton, Illinois, an antislavery editor, Elijah P. Lovejoy, was murdered by a mob that was attempting to destroy his printing press.

Two years after Garrison started publishing the *Liberator,* the American Anti-Slavery Society was formed and soon came under his influence. Garrison, however, refused to support political efforts at abolition because to him any constitution or political system that supported slavery was immoral. He also insisted on diluting the movement by supporting other causes such as women's rights, and he relied totally on moral persuasion to bring about change. Eventually, his abrasive character and stubborn principles led to a split in the society.

In 1840, abolitionists from the Midwest and western New York organized the American and Foreign Anti-Slavery Society, dividing the movement into two hostile camps. The prime movers of the new group were Theodore Dwight Weld, a propagandist for abolition, and Lewis and Arthur Tappan, who provided financial support. Many blacks outside the Garrisonian strongholds of Boston and Philadelphia joined them and supported the new political party they backed, the Liberty party.

Some of the abolitionists had the single-minded purpose of a Garrison or a Weld, but others, although they despised slavery, had small sympathy for black people. At best, some of them lacked courage. One admitted fear of offending his neighbors: "In walking with a colored brother, the darker the night, the better Abolitionist was I." Some questioned whether it was proper to admit blacks into antislavery societies, and many saw black people in patronizing stereotypes that were not much better than the views of the racists. Ellery Channing, a prominent abolitionist, wrote a tract describing black men as "affectionate, easily touched," and as having "meek, long-suffering, loving virtue." Another abolitionist advised Douglass: "Better have a little of the plantation speech than not; it is not best that you seem too learned."

Blacks chafed under this kind of patronizing support. The militant Martin R. Delany protested that antislavery societies "presumed to *think* for, dictate to, and *know* better what suited colored people, than they know for themselves." In the 1960s, when black civil rights workers challenged their liberal white supporters, they used the same language to protest what they considered to be domination. But the abolitionists, like white liberals of a later period, spoke out when all were silent and laid down their lives for the cause of justice. If some were not wholly with black people, body and soul, the majority offered their fortunes and their lives to the cause.

Douglass himself owed much to Garrison, of whom he said, "I stand in relation to him something like that of a child to a parent." But just as children eventually leave their parents' home, so, too, Douglass left Garrison. The first step in their break came when Douglass moved to Rochester, New York, to start printing the *North Star,* later to become *Frederick Douglass' Journal.* In 1849, Douglass told a Boston audience he would "welcome the intelligence . . . that the slaves had risen in the South, and that the sable arms which had been engaged in beautifying and adorning the South were engaged in spreading death and devastation there." This was a far cry from Garrison's pacifism. When Douglass became converted to the view that the Constitution was not wholly a proslavery document and that political activity was necessary, the break was final. Garrison felt betrayed, and the two men never spoke to each other again.

Douglass was not the only black leader in the abolitionist movement. One of the most uncompromising black spokesmen was the Rev. Henry Highland Garnet, who has been called the "Thomas Paine of the abolitionist movement." In 1843, he delivered a fiery address to the Buffalo, New York, meeting of the National Negro Convention, calling on all slaves to rise up against their masters. "There is not much hope of redemption without the shedding of blood," he declared. "If you must bleed, let it all come at once—rather die *freemen, than live to be the slaves."*

Garnet's call to arms echoed the earlier and perhaps more famous *Walker's Appeal,* issued in 1829 by David Walker, a Boston clothing dealer and agent for John Russwurm's newspaper, *Freedom's Journal.* Walker chilled slaveowners with his forthright attack on slavery and with his call for black men to strike for their freedom. He asked Americans: ". . . will you wait until we shall, under God, obtain our liberty by the crushing arm of power? Will it not be dreadful for you? I speak Americans for your own good. We must and shall be free I say, in spite of you." His advice to slaves—"kill or be killed." The appeal unleashed southern thunder: the mayor of Savannah wrote Boston's mayor asking that Walker be jailed, and four states enacted laws to prevent the publishing of similar "seditious" material.

One of the most famous and revered of the black abolitionists was a powerful, outspoken woman named Sojourner Truth. She was over six feet tall, and her sharp wit and barbed tongue held hecklers at bay, while she captivated countless audiences with moral fervor and prophetic preaching. Christened Isabella Baumfree, she changed her name to reflect her feeling that God had chosen her to "sojourn" across the land, spreading truth.

All over the country blacks took up the appeal for freedom and equality. The wealthy black Philadelphian James Forten organized antislavery societies and converted important abolitionists to the principle of racial equality and urged them to write off emigration as an answer to the black man's problems. William Wells Brown, one of America's first black novelists and playwrights and an historian of note, like Douglass, lectured against slavery in America and in England and was prominent in a number of reform movements. Alexander Crummell was not an abolitionist like the others—he was an agent for the Colonization Society—but he was one of the first to challenge doctrines of black inferiority militantly and to encourage racial self-confidence and pride.

Other black leaders founded groups to fight slavery in the South and discrimination in the North. Ohio blacks organized conventions to protest the Black Codes, laws that discriminated against their people, and eventually got them repealed in that state in 1849. In Boston, blacks joined with the Garrisonians in the successful fight to end segregation in schools and trains and to repeal bans on intermarriage.

Black men, laboring to end the degredation and slavery that afflicted their brothers in those dark days, were perhaps at their most effective as workers on the Underground Railroad. This informal network of black and white abolitionists helped slaves escape to the free cities of the North or to Canada. A Cincinnati Quaker, Levi Coffin, recalled: "We knew not what night or what hour of the night we would be roused from slumber by a gentle rap at the door. That was the signal announcing the arrival of a train of the Underground Railroad, for the locomotive did not whistle, nor make any unnecessary noise."

Coffin was responsible for safely shielding thousands of black runaways from the slave hunters. The story is told that a party of slave catchers from Kentucky spent weeks looking for a "train" of seventeen fugitives they knew to be in Coffin's neighborhood, but he spirited them away to safety. As the slave hunters left town, one is said to have pointed to Coffin's home and ruefully exclaimed: "There's an Underground Railroad around here and Levi Coffin is its president."

The railroad's "depots" covered the North, and false closets, trapdoors, and secret hiding places of all descriptions were built by the ingenious friends of the fugitives. A New York undertaker used his hearse to transport runaways across the border, and a bookbinder built a large wagon with a secret compartment for the same purpose. An

Ohio abolitionist designed his house with two secret rooms in which to hide fugitives. By 1855, it was estimated that sixty thousand slaves had traveled northward on the clandestine highways.

The act of running away was in itself terrifying, and only the certainty of such help enabled so many slaves to attempt it. Frederick Douglass wrote that when he was considering making his break for freedom, he and his companions saw more dangers than opportunities. "At every gate through which we had to pass," he wrote, "we saw a watchman, at every ferry a guard, on every bridge a sentinel, and in every wood a patrol or slave hunter. We were hemmed in on every side." Not surprisingly, Douglass's Rochester home was an important station on the Underground Railroad; at one time he sheltered eleven fugitives there while raising the money to get them safely across the border.

The greatest risks were taken by the "conductors" on the railroad. One of the most successful and daring of these was John Fairfield, a Virginian from a slaveholding family. He was a born actor and assumed many roles as he went south recruiting "passengers to freedom." Once he posed as a slave trader, and another time he took the part of a salt trader whose boats, instead of being filled with salt for sale downriver, were filled with slaves headed for Levi Coffin's station. In his most dramatic exploit he smuggled twenty-eight slaves to safety disguised as mourners in a funeral procession. Fairfield continued his activities for twelve years and is believed to have met death while helping to lead a slave rebellion in Tennessee.

Most of the conductors, however, were black. Elijah Anderson led more than a thousand of his black brothers out of the prison of slavery before he himself died in a Kentucky prison. Josiah Henson escaped from slavery and then set forth from his home in Canada to lead hundreds along freedom's road. Another fugitive who found a haven in Canada, John Mason, brought 265 slaves out of his native Kentucky within a nineteen-month period and helped nearly a thousand others in a perilous career that saw him captured and sold back into slavery, only to escape again.

The most famous of the railroad's black conductors was a slight, frail woman with the heart of a lion, Harriet Tubman. She carried a pistol, which she threatened to use against either slave catchers or slaves whose second thoughts about running away placed her escape parties in danger. She made nineteen trips into the slave kingdom, bringing more than three hundred souls northward. Appropriately called the "Moses of her people," she returned to the South during the Civil War to act as a nurse, guide, and spy for Union troops.

Slaves came north in a variety of ways: on foot, like Harriet Tubman who walked from Maryland to Pennsylvania; by sea, like the seven Florida slaves who escaped to the Bahamas in a small boat; and even by freight. In 1848, Henry (Box) Brown crawled into a trunk three feet long, two feet wide, and less than three feet deep and was mailed by a white friend. When the box arrived at the home of a Philadelphia agent of the Underground Railroad, the top was removed and Brown uncoiled himself after two days as human freight, free at last. One of the most famous escapes was that of William and Ellen Craft, a Georgia couple. Ellen took advantage of her fair complexion to pose as a sickly young man traveling with a slave servant (William). They told their story, as did Brown, to thousands of appreciative audiences all over the country and in England.

When the runaways reached northern cities, they were protected from recapture and re-enslavement by vigilance committees. Frederick Douglass, when he arrived in New Bedford, was assured that no slave catcher would dare to try to kidnap blacks from that town thanks to the militancy of its black population. And when a woman from Maryland arrived in Philadelphia to search for her escaped slaves, the vigilance committee plastered the city with posters warning them and exposing her mission.

Southerners, of course, did not sit idly by while the iron curtain of slavery was pierced by the far-flung lines of the Underground Railroad. In 1850, when the controversy over whether there should be slavery in the free territories of the West was intense, they succeeded in getting a strong fugitive slave law passed, one that made federal officers responsible for returning runaways to their masters. The law was part of what became known as the Compromise of 1850. The compromise was a patchwork of tidbits. The North gained California's entry into the Union as a free state and an end to the slave trade in the District of Columbia. The South got its Fugitive Slave Law and a federal hands-off policy regarding slavery in the new territories. The compromise ended the threat of secession and war —for a decade.

The Fugitive Slave Law stuck in the throats of the abolitionists. Frederick Douglass said: "The only way to make the Fugitive Slave Law a dead letter is to make half a dozen or more dead kidnappers. The man who takes the office of a bloodhound ought to be treated as a bloodhound."

Blacks in Christiana, Pennsylvania, took him at his word, and a slaveholder who came to town to steal back his former slaves lost his life in the attempt. Many northerners who had no quarrel with the slave system hated the new law. They resented the way it placed their local laws and officials at the service of slaveholders. Their resentment gave recruits to the abolitionists, whose lonely message found more and more supporters as the decade wore on.

Abolitionists stole some slaves back from the slave stealers. Shadrach, a fugitive in danger of re-enslavement, was spirited out of a Boston courtroom and across the border by a well-organized team of abolitionist commandos. But two other attempts failed. In 1851, Thomas Sims was returned to his Georgia master despite protests that brought out the militia. And in 1854, Anthony Burns was sent back to his Virginia master after an abolitionist raid on his Boston prison that cost the life of a policeman. Burns was escorted to the ship that was to carry him back to bondage by a battalion of cavalry, an artillery regiment, and several companies of marines. Two thousand soldiers guarded the lone black man as church bells tolled their farewell. Fifty thousand citizens, beneath a cannon pointing at them from the courthouse steps, hissed "Shame, shame, shame," while the mournful procession passed. Burns was the last slave Boston ever returned, law or no law.

The fugitive slave issue was just one way in which northerners felt the aggressive demands of the slaveholders of the South. It seemed to them that there was no containing the blight of slavery—short of war. The South, on the other hand, felt a need to expand its system. As a Georgia congressman stated: ". . . whenever slavery is confined within certain specified limits, its future existence is doomed." There were periodic proposals to annex Cuba and other areas in South and Central America. In 1854, *The Richmond Enquirer* editorialized in favor of developing the countries between the American slave states and the Amazon Valley with slave labor, and there were other similar proposals. When the United States went to war against Mexico in 1846, the campaign was very unpopular in the North, where it was rightly seen as an attempt to extend slavery into the Southwest.

The proud, powerful men of the slaveholding aristocracy could not consent to limits on slavery anywhere without admitting that the institution they considered the only proper foundation of civilization was inherently evil. Thus, they fought for slavery in the new western territories, even though the land was unsuited for the plantation labor on which the slave system thrived.

As the North became more impatient with the demands of the slavocracy, the South became more rigid. Even the mild misgivings of a Jefferson were considered treasonous by the 1830s, and the region limited free speech and suppressed every hint of dissent. Many states barred abolitionist literature, and in 1835 a Charleston, South Carolina, mob broke into the post office and made a bonfire of antislavery newspapers. One Georgian who subscribed to the *Liberator* was tarred and feathered, then burned and whipped. A white man in Virginia who had the temerity to state that "black men have, in the abstract, a right to their freedom," was whipped and run out of town. Arkansas, in 1850, made it a crime to "maintain that owners have not the right of property in their slaves."

Sometimes merely being from the North was enough to condemn a man. Two teachers in South Carolina were ordered to leave town, although, as a newspaper commented, "Nothing definite is known of their abolitionist or insurrectionary sentiments, but being from the North and therefore necessarily imbued with doctrines hostile to our institutions, their presence in this section has been obnoxious and at any rate suspicious." Even the proslavery president of the University of Mississippi was forced to resign because he had been born in the North.

Slavery, once considered a necessary evil, was now elevated to the supreme good. As John Calhoun declared in 1837, "Let me not be understood as admitting, even by implication, that the existing relations between the two races in the slaveholding states is an evil—far otherwise: I hold it to be a good, as it has thus far proved itself to be to both and will continue to prove so if not disturbed by the fell spirit of abolition." Southerners withdrew into a siege mentality that led them to defend slavery by hating freedom itself. As one Virginia editor wrote: "We have got to hating everything with the prefix *free*—from free Negroes up and down the whole catalogue—*free farms, free labor, free society* . . . and *free schools*—all belonging to the same brood of damnable *isms!"*

The dark night of hate and suppression fell upon the South as its ruling slaveholder class understood what many northerners didn't: that it was fighting for its life. The foundations of their power and the whole of their wealth lay in slavery. To limit slavery, to recommend gradual abolition, to encourage voluntary freeing of slaves by individual masters, to allow slaves to escape to the North—all these could open the door to northern money and northern industrial control. Slaveholders might have silenced the outcry by switching from a slave labor system to a system of paid labor. But they knew that such a change would encourage competition from northern moneyed interests and reduce them from a planter aristocracy to a managerial class, shorn of effective power and social standing.

The decade of the 1850s was torn by sectional bitterness and bloodshed. When Congress opened the territories west of the Mississippi to slavery with the Kansas-Nebraska Act of 1854, antislavery men from the North and slavery supporters from the South turned the state into a battleground. The town of Lawrence, Kansas, was sacked by armed settlers from the South, and John Brown led a band that struck back by killing five proslavery men at Pottawatomie. "Bleeding Kansas" became a northern battle cry as opposition to slavery mounted.

In the midst of this strife, a South Carolina congressman, Preston Brooks, visciously attacked the abolitionist Senator Charles Sumner of Massachusetts on the floor of the Senate while another southern congressman prevented interference, holding Sumner's friends off with a pistol. "I gave him about thirty first rate stripes," the fanatical Brooks said. "Toward the last he bellowed like a calf. I wore my cane out completely, but saved the Head which is gold." The attack resulted in a wave of indignation and pushed the divided country still closer to the war that seemed inevitable.

In 1857 the Supreme Court delivered a decision that seemed to prove to many northerners that the slavocracy was in solid control of all three of the major branches of the national government. Chief Justice Roger Taney ruled that Dred Scott, a slave who sued for freedom on the grounds that his master had taken him to a free territory, could not sue and had no standing in court because "people of African descent are not and cannot be citizens of the United States, and cannot sue in any court of the United States. . . ." Taney carried the logic of slaveowners to its ultimate conclusion, buttressing his argument by referring to the laws of various states that "show that a perpetual and impassible barrier was intended to be erected between the white race and the one which they had reduced to slavery, and governed as subjects with absolute and despotic power . . ."

Northerners were angered by the ruling of the southern-dominated Court, which affected the laws of their states. Like the Fugitive Slave Law, the Dred Scott decision seemed another thrust at them by the long arm of the slavocracy. Frederick Douglass said that the Dred Scott decision "may be one necessary link in the chain of events preparatory to the complete overthrow of the whole slave system." If so, yet another link remained to be forged, and it came in the person of the Kansas free-soil fighter, John Brown.

Brown became convinced that only a bold, daring attack on the stronghold of slavery itself would save the country. On October 16, 1859, Brown led a raiding party of twenty-one men, including his sons and five blacks, and captured the United States arsenal at Harpers Ferry, Virginia. The expedition was doomed to fail. Brown had hoped that his exploit would rouse the slaves to revolt, but there were few slaves in that part of Virginia, and his party was put to rout by marines under the command of Colonel

Robert E. Lee. Brown and a handful of his companions were captured, tried, and put to death.

When he heard the death sentence proclaimed, Brown told the court in words that electrified the North: "Now, if it is deemed necessary that I should forfeit my life for the furtherance of the ends of justice, and mingle my blood further with the blood of my children and with the blood of millions in this slave country whose rights are disregarded by wicked, cruel, and unjust enactments, I say, let it be done."

Brown's martyrdom supplied the needed link in the chain of events leading to civil war and emancipation. As his friend and admirer Frederick Douglass said years later: "When John Brown stretched forth his arm the sky was cleared—the time for compromise was gone—the armed hosts stood face to face over the chasm of a broken Union and the clash of arms was at hand."

9. The War of Liberation

On April 12, 1861, the predawn sky above the old port of Charleston, South Carolina, was lit by mortar fire. The big guns raged, belching smoke and ripping the air with the shrieks of exploding shells. Porches and rooftops were jammed with crowds of people watching the spectacle that signaled the start of a bloody civil war and, ultimately, the end of slavery. Thirty-four hours after the guns started firing, the harbor's federal fortress, Fort Sumter, surrendered. The shell-tattered Stars and Stripes was hauled down, and in its place the Stars and Bars of the Confederacy was hoisted.

The firebrands and diehards of the slavocracy had seceded from the Union. They turned their backs on the new government of President Abraham Lincoln in Washington and set up their own Confederate States of America, consisting of South Carolina, Mississippi, Florida, Alabama, Georgia, Louisiana, Texas, Arkansas, North Carolina, Virginia, and Tennessee. The rebel nation was pledged to maintain slavery and, as shown by the firing on Fort Sumter, to wipe out the federal presence on its soil.

The new nation was founded on hysteria. John

Brown's raid had thrown the slave states into panic, and now vigilante committees and armed gangs terrorized wide areas of the South. Everywhere, slave plots were discovered; everywhere, abolitionists were suspected of stirring rebellion. Twenty-three suspects were lynched in Mississippi. Charleston, according to the British consul there, was gripped in "a reign of terror." Yankees in Georgia, Louisiana, and South Carolina were beaten and driven from the state. An elderly Texas minister who believed slavery was a God-given blessing was whipped for criticizing bad treatment of slaves.

John Brown's ghost hovered over the Southland, but it was the election of Abraham Lincoln with less than 40 percent of the vote in a close race for the presidency that pushed the South to the suicidal brink of rebellion. When northern votes put the Republicans in office, the planters knew they were doomed to a gradual death. The Republicans were committed to blocking further extension of the slave system into the free territories. The South had to strike first. South Carolina led the way when in December, 1860, a state convention unanimously backed secession. Mississippi followed in January, then other states.

In March, the new president, gaunt and rigidly erect, strove to reassure the South of his intentions. "I have no purpose," Lincoln said in his Inaugural Address, "directly or indirectly, to interfere with the institution of slavery in the States where it exists. I believe I have no lawful right to do so, and I have no inclination to do so." But his words fell on deaf ears. Attempts at compromise also failed. The South preferred a life-and-death struggle to preserve its way of life. After the April 12 attack on Fort Sumter, there was

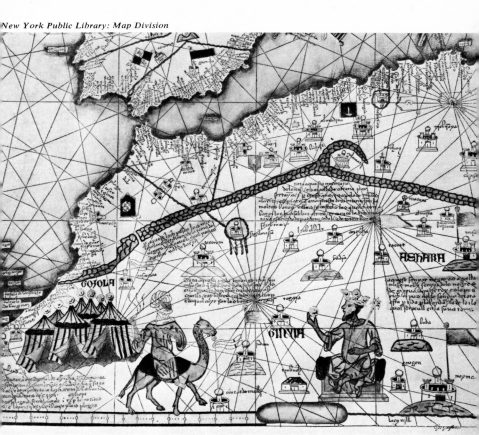

A fourteenth century Spanish map
of northwest Africa depicting Mali's king Mansa Musa
as the gold-rich sovereign of the Sahara

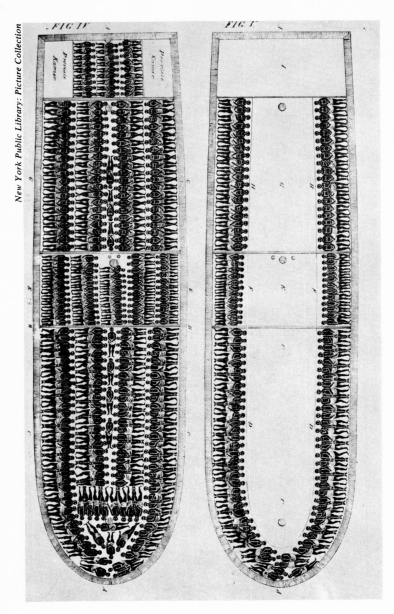

The loading plan of a slave ship

Black captives being lowered into the hold of a slave ship

A slave auction
in colonial America

Peter Salem shoots the British commander
at the battle of Bunker Hill

(Opposite page, bottom) The myth of the benevolent slave system can be seen in this idyllic picture of George Washington at his Mount Vernon plantation. *(Above)* In reality, the picture of the whip-bearing overseer on a Louisiana sugar plantation is closer to the truth.

The capture of Nat Turner, the most famous of slave rebels

Frederick Douglass,
an escaped slave
who became
a leader in the
abolition movement

Black troopers spearheading the Union attack on Fort Wagner

A Civil War recruiting poster

The old and the young crowded into the Freedmen's Bureau schools.

A black congressman speaks to the House of Representatives, 1869.

The
Ku Klux Klan
spread terror
in parts of the
South during
Reconstruction.

Field workers weighing their day's picking at the turn of the century

Booker T. Washington, founder of Tuskegee Institute
and influential black spokesman

W. E. B. Du Bois, an early leader in the NAACP
and editor of its magazine, *Crisis*

Marcus Garvey,
black
nationalist
of the
1920s

Mobs of civilians and police stoned and beat blacks
during the Chicago riot of 1919.

The Depression drove many blacks from the rural South to northern cities, where hard times forced many to live in shacks and hovels.

Black GI's in the South Pacific during World War II

United Press International

White mobs in Little Rock, Arkansas, tried to keep black children from attending previously all-white schools in 1957, and troops were called out to enforce the court's school desegregation order.

The Reverend Martin Luther King, Jr., addressing
the 1963 March on Washington

Malcolm X, a leading spokesman for black nationalism

no turning back. In May, Lincoln called for 500,000 volunteers, and the Civil War was on.

Black men rushed to volunteer to fight for the Union cause, but Lincoln refused to admit them into the lily-white ranks of the Army. Blacks formed drill companies in Boston, New York, and elsewhere and petitioned state legislatures and the War Department to be allowed to fight. Cincinnati blacks who organized a company of recruits were roughly told by the police: "We want you d—d niggers to keep out of this; this is a white man's war."

Ohio's governor, David Tod, answered black leader John Mercer Langston's offer to recruit black troops with a curt note. "Do you not know, Mr. Langston, that this is a *white* man's government; that white men are able to defend and protect it? . . . When we want you colored men, we will notify you."

And so it went. The patriotic rush to the colors by black citizens was met with insult and scorn, and Lincoln himself told delegations of blacks who came to plead for a chance to enlist that "if we were to arm [blacks], I fear that in a few weeks the arms would be in the hands of the rebels." He took a dim view of the black man's ability, and he was afraid that arming them would drive the still-loyal border states into the waiting arms of the Confederacy.

If northern blacks were stymied in their attempt to support the Union, southern blacks voted with their feet, fleeing to the Union lines in large numbers. At first, a handful filtered into Union camps in Virginia, but soon the trickle became a flood until everywhere that the northern armies penetrated in the South, black families joined them, seeking freedom.

When the Union Army marched into Louisiana, slaves from miles around flocked to the troops. "Every soldier had a Negro marching in the flanks, carrying his knapsack," the commanding general reported. Plantation carts, filled with black women and children and their belongings, were swamping his camp. . . . "I have a great many more Negroes in my camp now than I have whites."

The man General Ulysses S. Grant appointed to care for the refugees, the Rev. John Eaton, described the shocking condition of "the army of slaves and fugitives, pushing its way irresistably toward an army of fighting men . . . the women in travail, the helplessness of childhood and old age, the horrors of sickness and of frequent death."

The desertion of the slaves was a mighty blow to the Confederacy. The embattled secessionists depended on slave labor for their food supply, and the flight of the blacks—perhaps half a million people during the course of the war—crippled the southern economy.

The Union generals, though, had mixed feelings about the blacks streaming into their camps. Some actually wanted to return them to their masters as fugitive slaves. Some put them to work on Army-run plantations. Jefferson Davis's family plantation was turned over to nearly fifteen hundred blacks after its capture by Union troops. They raised corn, cotton, and vegetables, showing large profits and demonstrating the energy and ability of free men.

Often, however, the new freedom was little different from the old slavery. Many abandoned farms were leased by the Army to speculators who were supplied with black labor paid from $2.50 to $5 a month, from which clothing and supplies were deducted. A contemporary investigator said of the new masters: "The desire of gain alone prompts them, and they care little whether they make it out of the blood of those they employ or from the soil."

The refugee camps the Army set up were little better. Thousands were forced into overcrowded cabins, and disease swept through a population weakened by long, arduous journeys through Confederate lines and by poor diets and inadequate clothing.

The general attitude among federal officials was, in John Eaton's words, "bewilderment and panic, foreseeing the demoralization and infection of the Union soldiers and the downfall of the Union cause." More far-seeing commanders, however, realized that the refugees represented the means of victory. General David Hunter, in command of the sea islands off the southern coast, declared an end to slavery and assembled a black regiment, but Lincoln revoked Hunter's declaration of freedom and the War Department forced the general to dismiss his black soldiers. Black units were also raised in Kansas and New Orleans in defiance of federal orders.

It remained for Congress to act to help black people. Laws were passed freeing slaves in the territories and in the District of Columbia. Officers were forbidden to return fugitive slaves. Rebel lands were confiscated, and slaves who helped the Union were freed. At length, the President was given the power to enroll blacks into the armed forces. Yet Lincoln was not enthusiastic about this flurry of Congressional activity. He delayed raising black troops. He threatened to veto laws taking lands and property from the rebels. He forced Congress to pay $1,000,000 to the masters of slaves freed in the capital. He also had Congress set aside a fund to ship the freedmen out of the country.

This colonization project was dear to his heart. Convinced that together the races "suffer on each side," Lincoln was constantly looking for likely reservations, Panama, maybe, or Liberia, for resettling the blacks, whose forefathers had tilled the American soil. Once, Lincoln asked Frederick Douglass whether the freed black men should be allowed to remain in the United States. "Yes," answered Douglass with a twinkle in his eye, "they wouldn't take up more room than they do now." Nevertheless, days before his assassination, Lincoln was looking into the possibility of shipping the freedmen to Haiti.

Lincoln was no abolitionist, no radical in the sense that Garrison was called a radical. He believed in white supremacy: " . . . there must be the position of superior and inferior, and I as much as any other man am in favor of having the superior position assigned to the white race." He was no believer in equality: "I am not, nor ever have been in favor of bringing about the social and political equality of the white and black races." But Lincoln hated slavery, and he wanted some form of fair play for blacks. "I am naturally anti-slavery," he declared. "If slavery is not wrong, nothing is wrong." And he said: "All I ask for the Negro is that if you do not like him, let him alone. If God gave him but little, that little let him enjoy."

Above all, Lincoln felt that his duty as president was to restore the Union. Before the rebellion he was prepared to accept slavery, and he was prepared to let the South keep its evil institution if that would end the war. "My paramount object in this struggle," he wrote, "is to save the Union and is not either to save or to destroy slavery. . . . What I do about slavery, and the colored race, I do because I believe it helps to save the Union; and what I forbear, I forbear because I do not believe it would help save the Union."

In the late spring of 1862, Lincoln decided he must destroy slavery in order to save the Union. The war had been going badly, and he decided that only a drastic change of tactics would defeat the Confederacy. The time for emancipating the slaves was at hand.

One bright summer day, the President went to the telegraph office of the War Department, asked its head, Thomas T. Eckert, for pen and paper, seated himself at Eckert's desk, and began to write. "He would look out of the window a while," Eckert later wrote, "and then put his pen to paper, but he did not write much at once. He would study between times, and when he had made up his mind he would put down a line or two, and then sit quiet for a few minutes. After a time he would resume his writing . . ."

Throughout the summer, Lincoln would make his visits to Eckert's office, away from the noisy activity of the White House. He agonized over the wording of the document, waiting for a significant Union victory on the battlefield so that he could issue his proclamation from a position of strength. He had a long wait. The Union Armies, under feeble leadership, were not winning battles. But on September 17 word finally came that the federal troops had defeated the Confederates at Antietam, Maryland, and a week later Lincoln announced that he would free the slaves of the Confederacy on January 1, 1863. On the New Year Lincoln seated himself at his White House desk, took his gold pen, and, hands trembling, signed his name to the Emancipation Proclamation.

It was a feeble document, falling far short of the

sweeping measures sought by abolitionists and radical congressmen. It conferred freedom only on slaves held in the areas controlled by the rebels. The more than 800,000 blacks held in slavery in states loyal to the Union were not affected. The proclamation freed only those slaves beyond the reach of federal power. It was a war measure, designed to create unrest behind the enemy lines. And by injecting the moral issue of slavery into the Union's aims, Lincoln hoped to discourage foreign support of the Confederacy and to strengthen his position with the group of Congressional legislators called Radicals because of the position they took, extreme for those times. A London newspaper pointed out that Lincoln's proclamation meant "not that a human being cannot justly own another, but he cannot own him unless he is loyal to the United States."

By the war's end, only one in twenty of the four million slaves had won their liberty under the proclamation. And even these had won but a shaky freedom until the passage of the Thirteenth Amendment, which permanently ended slavery, for Lincoln still planned to introduce programs of compensated gradual emancipation after the war.

Despite its shortcomings, the Emancipation Proclamation was greeted with joyous acclaim by blacks throughout the North. At an all-night Boston meeting attended by abolitionist leaders, including Frederick Douglass, there was pandemonium at the news, with three thousand people letting go with everything "from shouts of praise to sobs and tears." Similar meetings in other cities were marked by bell-ringing, music, and one-hundred gun salutes. At the White House itself, throngs of blacks and whites paraded arm in arm before the gates, shouting their approval.

The War of Liberation

It was not, Douglass wrote, "a proclamation of liberty throughout the land, unto all the inhabitants thereof," but he recognized "in its spirit a life and power far beyond its letter. . . . I saw that its moral power would extend much further."

Blacks and whites alike realized that, whatever Lincoln's hesitations and caution, the proclamation was the first step toward a permanent cure for the cancer of slavery. Freedom's news passed along the grapevine of the slave South, in spite of the rebel efforts to keep it secret. Throughout the region, in snow-white cotton fields, in humble, rotting slave shacks, and in the "great houses" themselves, slaves whispered the news of the liberation and laid plans for escape to the Union lines.

Emancipation was greeted with somewhat less enthusiasm among northern workingmen, who feared the war's end would bring black equality and black competition for scarce jobs. War suppliers, financial speculators, and railroads were growing rich from the war, but the workingman scraped out an impoverished existence, and he was prepared to fight against justice for blacks if it was at his expense. A century later similar feelings would cause a "white backlash" among blue-collar workers afraid that their jobs would be taken over by blacks.

Rioters attacked black workers in many northern cities. Brooklyn, Buffalo, Detroit, and Philadelphia saw severe outbreaks of violence. But the worst riot occurred in New York City in July, 1863. It started as a protest against the new draft law, instituted because the Union army ranks had grown thin from mounting casualties and declining enlistments. Crowds gathered around the draft office in an ugly mood. They soon turned violent, and within hours fifty thousand people were rampaging through the city streets, killing, burning, and looting.

The mob's frenzy soon turned on blacks, who were seen as the cause of the war and of the draft. Crowds swept into the black ghettos, killing and burning as they went. The Colored Orphan Asylum with its twelve hundred blacks was attacked. The children were led to the safety of a nearby police station, making their way through streets clogged with the dead and wounded, passing under lampposts from which dangled black victims of the mob. After four days of destruction, order was finally restored. More than a thousand people had been killed, ten thousand injured. The enemies of freedom were not only those who wore gray uniforms and whistled Dixie.

The rage of the northern mobs was also present in the Army's ranks. In the Emancipation Proclamation Lincoln had finally acted to carry out the Congress's year-old laws permitting black enlistments, and the document contained a clause admitting blacks into the armed forces. The reaction of the troops was predictable. "We don't want to fight side and side with a nigger," one typical Union soldier wrote in a letter home. "We think we are too superior a race for that." But when the white soldiers realized that black troops would help them win the war and that every black man killed or wounded might mean a white man spared, they changed their tune. The new refrain was expressed by a popular ditty of the day:

"In battle's wild commotion
I shouldn't at all object

If Sambo's body should stop a ball
That was coming for me direct."

Black Army units were quickly raised. At long last, the black man's desire to fight for freedom was honored. Frederick Douglass, who had long pleaded for black soldiers to "march into the South and raise the banner of Emancipation among the slaves," joined other black leaders to lead recruitment drives. With an eye toward the postwar future, he issued calls to black men to join the Army, for, he wrote, "Liberty won only by white men will lose half its lustre." Furthermore, Douglass saw black soldiers as a way to ensure equality. "Once let the black man get upon his person the brass letters U.S.," he wrote, "let him get an eagle on his button, and a musket on his shoulder and bullets in his pocket, and there is no power on earth which can deny that he has earned the right to citizenship in the United States."

The small numbers of black troops in the Army were soon joined by many thousands more, and from early 1863 to the end of the war few battles were fought in which blacks did not see action.

The doubts many Union officers felt about the fighting ability of blacks quickly vanished. In early 1863 black soldiers led by the Massachusetts abolitionist, Thomas Wentworth Higginson, raided Confederate territory off the Georgia coast. Higginson found them superior to white troops because "instead of leaving their homes and families to fight they are fighting for their homes and families, and they show the resolution and sagacity which a personal purpose gives. It would have been madness to attempt, with the bravest white troops, what I have successfully accomplished with black ones."

Other Union officers came to share Higginson's opinion. The turning point was the battle of Port Hudson, a Confederate strongpoint on the lower Mississippi. In May, 1863, Union troops, including regiments of Louisiana blacks, made a suicidal assault on the heavily defended post. Withering fire from the Confederate batteries drove them off, but the black troops had shown an extraordinary courage and skill. "You have no idea how my prejudices with regard to Negro troops have been dispelled by the battle," wrote one officer. "The brigade of Negroes behaved magnificently and fought splendidly; could not have done better. They are far superior in discipline to white troops, and just as brave."

Black troops served in the trenches, sailed in the Navy, rode in the cavalry. They built bridges and fortifications. Spies such as Harriet Tubman and James Lawson went behind the enemy's lines and brought back valuable information. Slaves in the South served as the eyes and ears of the Union's spy network, and some performed heroic deeds of sabotage and daring. One man, Robert Smalls, a slave sailor on the Confederate gunboat *The Planter,* raised the Confederate flag over the ship and silently sailed it out of Charleston harbor. Once at sea, he hauled down the flag and surrendered the ship to the federal fleet. Smalls became a captain in the U.S. Navy, in command of the ship he so brilliantly navigated to freedom.

Although they fought well and bravely, black troops were discriminated against. They were nearly always led by white officers. In spite of the pleas of black leaders that commissions be given to blacks, the War Department refused. In all, less than a hundred black men were made officers during the course of the war. Even worse was the Army's policy of paying black soldiers less than whites. Blacks were paid $7 a month with $3 a month extra for clothing. White soldiers got $13 a month plus a $3.50 clothing allowance.

Blacks protested this discrimination bitterly; Douglass even took the subject up with Lincoln in a White House meeting. One regiment, from Massachusetts, refused to take any payment at all, rather than accept discriminatory wages. It was not until the last months of the war that Congress passed a bill granting equal pay.

Black soldiers were also singled out for special discrimination by the enemy. The Confederate Congress passed a law in 1863 providing that black soldiers captured in battle were to be treated according to the laws of the state in which they were captured. This meant death or sale into slavery. Confederate soldiers often refused to take black prisoners, and many were killed in cold blood. In April, 1864, rebel troops overran Fort Pillow, the Union garrison on the Mississippi River. Dozens of black soldiers were murdered after the fort's surrender, and for months afterward black soldiers went into battle crying, "Remember Fort Pillow."

The tough black troopers were the cutting edge of the Union forces, making the difference between victory and defeat in many a battle. More than 180,000 blacks served in the Union forces, over half of them recruited from the slave states. By war's end there were a hundred and twenty black infantry regiments, twenty-two artillery regiments, and seven regiments of cavalry. Thirty-eight thousand black soldiers were killed, and total casualties were more than a third of the total forces. Twenty-one blacks won the coveted Congressional Medal of Honor, the nation's highest military award.

By late 1864, the Confederacy seemed doomed to go down in defeat. Sherman's armies were marching through the South's heartland, slicing it in two, and Grant's armies were pressing the northern front hard. More and more rebel soldiers were deserting, and commanders complained of a lack of manpower. In desperation, the Confederates considered arming their slaves, promising eventual freedom in exchange for loyal combat. "We should employ them without delay," wrote General Robert E. Lee, and in the dying days of the war, the Confederates started to recruit black soldiers. They never saw action, however; the war ended too quickly.

The southern forces did use slaves as laborers, servants, teamsters, and workers on fortifications. Early in the war slaves were drafted for military labor, and some Confederate states forced free blacks back into slavery to provide badly needed manpower. But the victims of these acts were, by Dixie's standards, unreliable. Sabotage and spying were common, and when Union forces approached, blacks dropped their tools and fled to the armies of liberation.

The southerner's cause suffered from a fatal weakness. In their midst were four million blacks whose loyalties were to the enemy. Throughout the war, the South was crippled by fear of slave revolts and the need to divert scarce manpower to protect homes and fields from angry blacks. Men who could have been on the front lines fighting federal troops were, instead, patrolling the plantations. One Mississippian, pleading for more troops for this home guard, wrote that if there are "any more men taken out of this country, we may as well give it to the Negroes . . . now we have to patrole [sic] every night to keep them down."

Every step of the war was followed anxiously by the blacks in bondage. News spread rapidly in whispered conversations and secret meetings. Blacks used code words to carry on conversations about the war in front of their masters, and even in the most remote plantations, slaves offered up prayers for Abraham Lincoln and the federal armies. "The spirits of the colored citizens rise and fall with the ebb and flow of this tide of blue devils," wrote a Chattanooga editor, "and when they are glad as larks, the whites are depressed and go about the streets like mourners."

As the war drew to a successful close, the slaves no longer had to hide their joy. The first Union troops to march into Charleston were the battle-hardened veterans of the Twenty-first U.S. Colored Infantry. They were greeted by thousands of blacks, bursting with pride at seeing resplendent black soldiers in the blue uniforms of the republic. "Cheers, blessings, prayers, and songs were heard on every side," reported an observer. "Men and women crowded to shake hands with men and officers. . . . On through the streets of the rebel city passed the column, on through the chief seat of that slave power, tottering to its fall. Its walls rung to the chorus of manly voices singing 'John Brown,' 'Babylon is Falling,' and the 'Battle-Cry of Freedom'; while, at intervals, the national airs, long unheard there, were played by the regimental band. The glory and triumph of this hour may be imagined, but can never be described."

The Union victory meant the end of slavery. On plantations across the South, masters sorrowfully summoned their slaves to the "big house" to tell them "you are free, just as free as me or anybody else that's white." Their prayers for deliverance from the house of bondage had been answered. Free at last. No more chains. No more whips. No more to be sold like cattle. The freedmen heard the halting words of their former masters, who had owned their labor, their bodies, and their souls. Sometimes they listened in stunned silence; sometimes they exploded in wild ecstasy. Many a black mother across the South, like Booker T. Washington's mother, "leaned over and kissed her children while tears of joy ran down her cheeks."

10. Free at Last

The war was over. The southern countryside, according to Carl Schurz, presidential fact-finder, "looked for many miles like a broad black streak of ruin and desolation —the fences all gone; lonesome smoke stacks, surrounded by dark heaps of ashes and cinders, marking the spots where human habitations had stood; the fields along the road wildly overgrown by weeds, with here and there a sickly patch of cotton or corn cultivated by Negro squatters."

Hunger and disease stalked the new freedmen. "As a rule," a Union officer wrote, "they are hungry, naked, foot-sore . . . homeless and friendless." Some blacks left the plantations where they had been born and had toiled in bondage all their lives. They looked for work in the towns or on other farms. But most stayed put, replacing the slavery of the past with a new form of slavery, laboring for starvation-level wages. Diehard rebels were sure that blacks, freed from the not-so-loving care of their masters, would soon perish. "The child is already born who will behold the last Negro in the state of Mississippi," a Natchez newspaper confidently predicted.

If freedom was ever to have meaning, the black man needed equal political and economic rights, and that was what he now demanded. "We are men," proclaimed a national convention of black leaders, "and want to be as free in our native country as other men." A convention of freedmen in Virginia complained they were "sheep in the midst of wolves," and that "the only salvation for us . . . is in the possession of the ballot. Give us this and we will protect ourselves."

Economic independence was as essential as political liberty. "Every colored man will be a slave, and feel himself a slave," said a black army sergeant, "until he can raise his own bale of cotton and put his mark upon it and say 'this is mine.' " Blacks dreamed of "forty acres and a mule," the promise of their own land and the independence that would come with it. For some, the dream came true—briefly.

More than forty thousand were settled in South Carolina on former rebel lands that had been siezed by the government. One Confederate officer, returning to his plantation after the war, found it divided into family farms and settled by former slaves. "We own this land now," they told him. "Put it out of your head that it will ever be yours again." They were wrong. President Andrew Johnson reversed the policy. The freedmen were driven from the land by troops and forced once more into gang labor on the restored plantations.

If the government was unwilling to provide blacks with land, it did provide work, relief, and education. During the war, these services were in the hands of the Army and private charitable groups, including black organizations, that sent teachers and volunteers down south to help the freedmen. The enormous scale of the postwar problems, however, led Congress to establish the Freedmen's Bureau to coordinate the government's efforts in bringing stability to the southern black population.

The bureau sought to protect black workers by suggesting wage scales and overseeing contracts between freedmen and their employers. In practice, though, this made little difference on most plantations. The harried agents of the bureau were too few and too overworked to be effective. And the bureau's policy itself discriminated against blacks; any freedman who refused to contract for his labor or who could not find work was forced to labor on a bureau farm or on public works.

The bureau's relief work was more successful. It distributed food to white and black refugees; it set up more than 40 hospitals and treated 450,000 sick people. And it helped to settle more than 30,000 people uprooted from their homes by the war.

Most successful of all were the bureau's education programs. Some of today's best-known black colleges, such as Howard, Atlanta, and Fisk Universities, were aided. About a quarter of a million blacks of all ages were enrolled in its more than four thousand schools. As Booker T. Washington later wrote, "It was a whole race trying to go to school. Few were too young, and none too old, to make the attempt to learn. As fast as any kind of teachers could be secured, not only were day-schools filled, but night-schools as well."

The Freedmen's Bureau could have revolutionized American life. If it had been given the funds and the power to redistribute plantation land to the freed slaves, if it had been given broader authority to ensure their civil rights and to expand educational programs, the history of the nation would have followed a different and more democratic course. But history is full of "ifs." White citizens of the post-Civil War era had neither the interest nor the desire to bring full equality to the people they had enslaved for so long. Like the so-called "war on poverty" a century later, what the Freedmen's Bureau accomplished was mainly a holding operation, a short-term program to deal with an emergency situation, and not a broad attack on the basic problems of the society. The bureau was discontinued in 1869, after four brief years of work. Throughout its short life it was hampered by the hostility of southern racists and the indifference of northern politicians.

Lincoln's plan for the postwar South was extremely lenient. He wanted the rebel states back in the Union as quickly as possible. He would pardon Confederates who took an oath of allegiance to the U.S. Constitution and promised to accept federal actions on slavery. As soon as one-tenth of a state's voters took the oath, they could organize a state government, the military would be withdrawn, and the state would be in the Union again.

Congress passed a bill requiring much stiffer terms, but Lincoln killed it, saying: "It rejects the Christian principle of forgiveness in terms of repentance. I think it is enough if the man does no wrong hereafter." Which was like letting the wolf go free after it had promised not to kill any more chickens.

Lincoln was murdered before his policy could go into effect, but his successor, Andrew Johnson, a Tennessee Democrat, shared his views. The Freedmen's Bureau, for example, was established over President Johnson's veto. Like Lincoln, he had no intention of tearing apart the South's social structure and putting it back together again in a way that would bring equality to blacks.

He embarked on a soft Reconstruction policy. Pardons to rebel leaders flowed freely, and soon they were back in power, as if no blood had ever been spilled in the bitter Civil War. When the Thirty-ninth Congress met in December 1865, it included seventy-nine men who had been top Confederate leaders earlier in the year. In the southern states, the rebels, who had lost the war, were clearly winning the peace.

What rebel control of the South meant for blacks was summed up by a North Carolinian, who warned: "God have mercy on the blacks, if they are turned over to the government of their old masters, who seem determined to prove emancipation a curse." Their "old masters" were also determined to reduce the freedmen to a state of semislavery. Wages for black farm laborers were often as low as $10 a month. Ironically, if the black man owned a horse, he got $5 a month more for the use of the animal.

Violence was common. "Some planters held back their former slaves on their plantations by brute force," reported Carl Schurz. "Armed bands of white men patrolled the country roads to drive back the Negroes wandering about. Dead bodies of murdered Negroes were found on and near the highways and by-paths. Gruesome reports came from the hospitals. . . . A veritable reign of terror prevailed in many parts of the South."

The official policy of the southern states was summed up by a governor of Mississippi, who said, "Ours is, and it shall ever be, a government of white men." This policy was reflected in state laws that became known as the Black Codes. Like the old Slave Codes, they regulated the behavior of blacks. The codes gave blacks certain minimal legal rights, but their basic provisions were designed to keep the black man "in his place."

The laws varied from state to state, but most established racial segregation, kept blacks off juries, demanded special licenses for nonagricultural labor, and provided that unemployed blacks could be arrested and auctioned off to landowners. Mississippi barred blacks from buying or renting farm land. Louisiana's law forced blacks to sign labor contracts at the beginning of the year and forbade them to leave their jobs. Refusal to sign a contract meant arrest and forced labor with no pay. Mississippi, leaving no doubt that the aim of its code was virtual re-enslavement, added a section providing that the old criminal laws regulating slaves now applied to the freedmen.

The North, fresh from what it had thought was victory over the rebels, was infuriated by these laws. The last straw came when southern cities erupted in mass rioting against blacks. In Memphis, forty-six blacks were killed and eighty wounded. A New Orleans riot that was described as "an absolute massacre by the police . . . a murder which the mayor and police . . . perpetrated without any shadow of necessity," claimed thirty-four blacks dead and more than two hundred injured.

Andrew Johnson's policy had failed disastrously. More and more, it was obvious that he had become a prisoner of the South, as when he referred to the oppressive Black Codes as "measures . . . to confer upon freedmen the privileges which are essential to their comfort, protection, and security." An unruly Congress was insisting on control of Reconstruction policy, and Johnson rapidly lost public support by his wild attacks on Congressional leaders. Referring to the fact that he came to office through the death of Lincoln, people began calling him "His Accidency, the President."

The Republicans, who dominated the Congress, and especially the group known as the Radicals, took control of Reconstruction policy. They launched a successful effort to bring about black equality, black voting, and Republican domination of the South. Their aims were to give the black man the tools of freedom and thus to keep the Republican party in power by preventing former secessionists from controlling the Union through their votes in Congress.

Many Radical leaders were men of strong moral purpose. Representative Thaddeus Stevens of Pennsylvania told his district's voters, "I care not what you may say of Negro equality. I care not what you may say of radicalism; these are my principles, and with the help of God I shall die with them." He did. Upon his death, he was buried, at his own request, in a black cemetery as a protest against segregation. His headstone bore the words: "I have chosen this that I might illustrate in my death the principles which I advocated through a long life, Equality of Man before his Creator." Stevens had actively sought to bring about a true social revolution in the South. He drafted a bill to break up large plantations and provide every newly freed family with a forty-acre farm and $50. But Congress—and the nation —was not prepared to go that far, and the bill was defeated.

The Radicals did push through Congress, often over Johnson's vetoes, a series of laws that reconstructed southern states and protected the black man. In 1867, Congressional Reconstruction disbanded the Johnson-backed state governments and divided the South into military districts. The former rebel states had to fulfill strict requirements before they could rejoin the Union. There had to be constitutional conventions, with delegates elected by blacks and all whites who took an "iron-clad" oath of loyalty. The new state constitutions had to provide for black suffrage and be ratified by popular vote. Then the state had to ratify the Fourteenth Amendment, which granted citizenship and civil rights to all freedmen.

A series of federal laws was now passed to protect blacks. The 1866 Civil Rights Act guaranteed "full and equal benefit of all laws and proceedings for the security of person and property, as is enjoyed by white citizens." This wiped out the vicious Black Codes. Other laws protected the black man's right to vote, restricted voting by whites who had supported the rebellion, and prohibited discrimination and intimidation in voting. In 1875, the last of the measures passed was another Civil Rights Act that barred discrimination in public places such as inns, trains, and restaurants. Its language was similar to the language of the landmark Civil Rights Act of 1964 during the "second Reconstruction" a century later.

Three new Constitutional amendments were passed. The thirteenth, which went into effect in 1865, abolished slavery. The fourteenth, passed in 1868, with its broad federal guarantees of the rights of citizens, became the basis for most action on civil rights in later years. The last of the historic amendments, the fifteenth, was passed in 1870 and protected the right to vote. This actually benefited northern blacks more than the freedmen. Thanks to Congressional Reconstruction, southern blacks had the vote, but until ratification of the amendment most northern states had barred blacks from the ballot.

Our view of the South during Reconstruction has been blurred by persistent myths. The popular belief is that a vindictive Congress imposed military rule on the suffering South, creating governments dominated by ignorant blacks and their carpetbagger friends who looted state treasuries and oppressed southern whites. Nothing could be farther from the truth.

Military rule, for example, lasted a scant year or so, and few federal troops were ever stationed in the South. By 1868, almost all of the states under Congressional Reconstruction had civilian governments and were free of federal control. Reconstruction itself lasted for only a brief time. Radical Republican governments were in power for only three years in two states, and for as long as ten years in only three. Virginia, the capital of the Confederacy, never experienced Radical rule at all.

The state conventions formed to draft new constitutions were overwhelmingly white, although several states had black majorities in their population. Only eighteen of Alabama's 108 convention delegates were black; fifteen of North Carolina's 133; eight of Arkansas' 66. Blacks were in the majority only in the South Carolina delegation. For almost all of the states, native-born whites formed the largest single group of delegates.

The constitutions that emerged from these conventions

151

were the most democratic in the South's history. They provided for equality under the law. They broadened voting rights, eliminated property qualifications for office-holding and jury service, expanded public welfare, and created public school systems. South Carolina's constitution provided, for the first time, for popular election of the governor. Louisiana's provided for an integrated school system, and, for a time, New Orleans had integrated schools.

The state governments, like the conventions, functioned as coalitions of southern whites, northern migrants, and blacks. The myth that the governments of the Reconstruction South were under black domination doesn't stand up to the facts.

Blacks were always a minority in almost all of the state legislatures, and few held top statewide elective offices. There were no black governors, with the possible exception of P. B. S. Pinchback, Louisiana's lieutenant-governor, who was acting governor for a short seven weeks in 1872. There were only two black United States senators, Hiram Revels and Blanche Bruce, both from Mississippi. Blacks often held appointed offices and many local and county offices, but rarely in proportion to their numbers. Still, black officials made important contributions to southern governments of the time. It was not until the late 1960s that blacks would fill southern government posts again, and never in such numbers.

In part, blacks were cautious about using their new political power because they realized that few of their number were sufficiently educated to fill high posts. There was also a deep desire for reconciliation with white southerners and an understanding that cooperation was necessary to rebuild a new and better society. Typical was Beverly Nash, a black delegate to South Carolina's convention, who pointed to a banner emblazoned with the words, "United we stand, divided we fall," and painted a vision of a bright future represented by "the white man and the black man standing with their arms locked together, as the type of friendship and union which we desire."

Many whites came to accept the presence of their former slaves in places of responsibility. Blacks appeared at the polls, on the judges' benches, and in legislative councils with scarcely a murmur from whites. "It is amazing," wrote a North Carolinian, "how quietly our people take . . . Negroes on juries." More amazing was the way whites accepted desegregation of street cars and railroad cars. Just after the war, blacks in New Orleans, Richmond, Charleston, and other cities demonstrated and conducted "sit-ins" typical of the modern civil rights movement, to end segregation on public vehicles. Now, with the backing of the law, blacks were free to ride and go where they wished. Still, the new governments moved slowly when it came to social equality. Some segregation was common, especially in hotels, eating places, and schools.

Perhaps the greatest single accomplishment of the Reconstruction governments was that they established free public school systems, including schools for black children in states where teaching blacks to read and write had been a serious crime a few short years before. In addition, they built roads, hospitals, bridges, and asylums, all of which cost money, of course. Taxes and state debt rose sharply, especially compared to prewar state spending, which did not provide for the vital educational and social services that were instituted by the Reconstruction governments. These things are taken for granted today, but to the southern conservative of 1870, they were a waste of tax money on radical and dangerous schemes.

Some of the spending reflected the graft and corruption of the times, but it is a myth to say that Reconstruction governments were corrupt. Stealing was so widespread in the prewar South that a treasury agent recommended that a Mississippi official who stole $55,000 (his predecessor had stolen $100,000) be continued in his post as "another receiver would probably follow in the footsteps of the two." The treasurer of the Democratic Mississippi regime that overthrew the radical Republicans in 1875 embezzled $316,000, and other states had similar experiences. Louisiana's treasurer made off with more than a million dollars, and seven other state treasurers stole public monies in the decade following the Republicans' loss of power.

Postwar America was in a free-wheeling mood of expansion, and public standards of morality were low. In New York, the Tweed Ring was stealing about $100 *million,* Wall Street financiers robbed investors, and their speculations drove the country into a financial depression. In Washington, government corruption reached into the Cabinet and the Vice President's office. By these standards, the new governments of the South were models of honesty. Bribery and corruption, however, did thrive in some places. The railroads in Florida, Alabama, and other states were the big culprits, often bribing legislators to get state money, land, and credit to rebuild their lines. Often these railroads were headed by ex-Confederates and northern financiers, while white conservatives and Democrats, as well as blacks and Republicans, shared in the booty.

By and large, though, the Reconstruction governments provided a pause in the widespread thefts by state officials that marked previous and later regimes. Only a handful of state officials were caught with their hands in the till, even after their opponents came to power and painstakingly searched for evidence that would embarrass them. In general, black officeholders were of high caliber and included some of the most outstanding men of the age. Blanche K. Bruce, for example, the only Negro to be elected to a full term in the United States Senate until Edward Brooke's 1966 election, was born a slave. He became a power in the Senate, was considered for a Cabinet post, and held several high federal offices. "I am a Negro, and proud of my race," he would tell Washington society, which was impressed by his urbane manner. Another black man, John R. Lynch, rose from slavery to become speaker of the Mississippi House in his twenties and a three-term congressman after that. He was a spellbinding orator, and opponents feared to debate him. He later became an Army major and eventually an outstanding lawyer and political leader in Chicago.

The accomplishments of these and other black lawmakers is even more impressive when we consider that most of them grew up in slave cabins, were denied even the simplest education, and forced to toil in the field from sunrise to sundown. Few were as fortunate as South Carolina's state treasurer, Francis L. Cardozo, a minister and school principal, who had been educated abroad, or J. J. Wright, who joined that state's supreme court after long experience as a lawyer in the North. Far more common were people like Congressman Robert Smalls, the wartime naval hero, and other self-educated black leaders who built the coalition with white liberals that was to bring a brief period of sunlight into the gloomy dungeons of southern politics.

One of these whites, Albion Tourgée, wrote the following about the deeds of the black-supported state governments: "They instituted a public school system in a realm where public schools had been unknown. They opened the ballot-box and jury box to thousands of white men who had been debarred from them by a lack of earthly possessions. They introduced home rule in the South. They abolished the whipping post, and branding iron, the stocks and other barbarous forms of punishment which had up to that time prevailed. They reduced capital felonies from about twenty to two or three. In an age of extravagance they were extravagant in the sums appropriated for public works. In all that time, no man's rights of person were invaded under the forms of laws."

11. Jim Crow Rides High

Reconstruction could not kill the spirit of southern rebellion. It smoldered under the hot Dixie sun, flaring into occasional violence and gathering strength for a time when it could once more dominate the South and restore the black man to an inferior place in a racist system.

Vengeance rode at night. Under cover of darkness, white men donned sheets and hoods and rode the paths of the backwoods, leaving grim destruction behind them. Dawn's rays found the bullet-riddled body of a black man afloat in the swampy waters of a mud-clogged stream; a federal agent moaning in pain deep in a clump of woods, his whip-seared back a bloody mass; the house of a black tenant farmer burned to the ground, yellow flames licking at the last of his few possessions. This was the South's answer to Reconstruction and the civil rights of black men.

It began shortly after the war's end, in late 1865, when former rebels in Tennessee banded together in a secret organization that became known as the Ku Klux Klan. The aims of the Klan were expressed by one newspaper editor who counseled: "If to every tree in our forest-like streets were attached a rope; and to the ends of each rope a Northern and Southern Radical . . . then might we once more live in peace and harmony."

Within months, Ku Klux Klan chapters spread across the South. Often they were known by other names—Knights of the Camillia, Knights of the Rising Sun, The White League—but their aims and activities were the same: to spread terror among black people and any whites who dared treat blacks as equals. One such gang in Mississippi, called Heggie's Scouts, claimed credit for choking the Tallahatchie River with the bodies of 116 murdered blacks. In the first half of 1870, the Klan in only one South Carolina county murdered six men and whipped more than three hundred others.

By the early 1870s, despite federal and state actions to punish the terrorists, violence had become a successful political tool in the hands of conservative southerners. Through a combination of violence, economic and social pressures against black and white Republicans, and outright fraud, the South was returned to Democratic party rule and racist domination.

Mississippi's counter-revolution of 1875 took as its slogan: "Carry the election peaceably if we can, forcibly if we must." Hoping to rid the state of Republicans before the election, Mississippi newspapers printed the names of white party members and instructed readers to avoid social contact with them. One prominent Republican who resigned from his party explained to a black friend: "No white man can live in the South in the future and act with any other than the Democratic party unless he is willing and prepared to live a life of social isolation and remain in political oblivion."

Democratic "clubs" were organized throughout the state of Mississippi and armed with the latest rifles. They staged military parades to intimidate blacks and often went into action to wrest control from local Republicans. Carefully staged "riots" kept blacks in terror of exercising their right to vote. Thirty-five were killed in Vicksburg in 1874, and violence erupted throughout the state as the elections approached. Opposition meetings were broken up, speakers threatened and beaten, and polling booths surrounded by pistol-firing gangs.

When the smoke cleared, the Democrats had swept the state, Reconstruction was ended, and Mississippi once more had what one newspaper urged: "A white man's Government, by white men, for the benefit of white men."

Rule by the gun was tried elsewhere, too. Political murders became a way of life in Louisiana after fifty-nine blacks were killed at Colfax in 1873. A year later, the New Orleans White League took over the city, fighting off more than four thousand militiamen, policemen, and Army troops.

South Carolina's Democrats, called "Red Shirts" because of the uniforms they wore in public, instructed members to "control the vote of at least one Negro, by intimidation, purchase, keeping him away, or as each individual may determine how he may best accomplish it." Members were also cautioned that if a victim "deserves to be threatened, the necessities of the times require that he should die. A dead Radical is very harmless . . ."

The federal government stood idly by as Reconstruction was overthrown in most southern states. An appeal by Mississippi's governor for federal troops to end the election violence was refused by an irritated President Grant, who declared: "The whole public are tired of the annual autumnal outbreaks in the South."

The North *was* tired. The energies it had invested in a bitter war and in a period of intensive social reform were spent. In the presidential election of 1876, the Democrat Samuel J. Tilden, promising an end to Reconstruction, outpolled the Republican standard-bearer Rutherford B. Hayes by nearly 300,000 votes. But twenty votes in the Electoral College were in dispute, because of charges and countercharges of ballot-stealing. Tilden needed only one of these twenty votes to win, while Hayes needed a clean sweep. When a special commission awarded all the votes to Hayes, Democrats erupted in anger, and the nation was in the grip of a severe Constitutional crisis.

Hayes and his supporters, however, calmed the outcry by pursuing a "southern strategy" to woo Dixie Democrats away from their party. They promised federal subsidies for southern railroads, withdrawal of the few troops left in the South, political jobs for southern Democrats, and a hands-off policy in southern domestic affairs. In return, the southern Democrats supported Hayes and promised to be fair to the blacks whom he abandoned to their care. This compromise of 1877 saved the presidency for Hayes, but it ended Reconstruction and doomed the black man to a second-class citizenship that was to be his lot for nearly a century afterward.

The South's new leaders were willing to protect the black man as long as they could control his vote. Their aim was to help business prosper, and this meant exploitation of the poor of both races. Taxes and school budgets were cut, and state aid flowed to railroads and other businesses. Blacks were allowed to keep some of the political and social rights they had won during Reconstruction, but the price was poverty—grinding, degrading poverty.

Barred from employment in the textile mills that were springing up throughout the South, the black man was also losing higher paying skilled jobs. He was chained to the land, but the land he worked was rarely his own. Three out of four black farmers were tenants or sharecroppers, totally dependent on white planters. Wages for laborers were at the starvation level, and sharecroppers, who farmed the land in return for giving the landlord a share of the crop, were kept in virtual bondage by debts and high credit charges.

Cash rarely changed hands. The planter would advance seed, equipment, and mules to the sharecropper. During the year, groceries would be bought on credit at the local store, which was often also owned by the planter, who charged high prices and high interest rates. By the time crops were harvested and accounts settled, the farmer would find himself owing money to the planter. The debts would be charged against the next year's crop, when the whole cycle would start again, plunging the farmer deeper and deeper into a perpetual debt from which there was no escape.

But even the evils of sharecropping were preferable to the chain gang and the notorious convict-lease system. Trivial offenses were punished by long prison terms, creating a large supply of convicts whom states and counties leased to private corporations and planters. Prisoners were kept in huge rolling cages that were moved from job site to job site, or in rotting shacks deep in swamp areas. Chained together, black convicts built roads, worked in mines and turpentine flats, and farmed the huge plantations.

Prison camp conditions were inhuman; they lacked only gas ovens to be duplicates of the Nazi concentration camps of World War II. Sadistic guards, poor food, and disease were equally merciless. A Mississippi grand jury investigating conditions in a prison hospital reported that most of the convicts "have their backs cut in great wales, scars and blisters, some with the skin peeling off in pieces as the result of severe beatings. . . . They were lying there dying, some of them on bare boards, so poor and emaciated that their bones almost came through their skin, many complaining for want of food." In 1881, it was reported that the death rate among Arkansas's prisoners was 25 percent.

Fortunes were built on this slave labor. Politicians, judges, and prison wardens grew rich from payoffs by individuals and corporations who contracted for leases of convicts. And the "employers" made enormous profits from convict labor that cost only pennies a day in payments to the state.

The competition of prison labor meant low wages for free workers of both races. These people were kept down because the South wanted to attract new industries. Companies were seduced southward by descriptions of the "large body of strong, hearty, active, docile and easily contented Negro laborers . . . contented with their wages." Promises were made that "long hours of labor and moderate wages will continue to be the rule for many years to come."

These exploitative policies, coupled with hard times for farmers and a cycle of economic depressions that plagued the nation through the last decades of the nineteenth century, inspired a new militancy among workers. White farmers in the South and West formed the Farmers' Alliance, and a million blacks joined the Colored Farmers' Alliance. A national third party, the Populist party, was formed, and for a time the racial barriers were breached as whites and blacks were joined together in common purpose.

Georgia's Populist leader, Tom Watson, called for a united front, saying: "You are kept apart that you may be separately fleeced of your earnings. You are made to hate each other because upon that hatred is rested the keystone of the arch of financial despotism which enslaves you both. You are deceived and blinded that you may not see how this race antagonism perpetuates a monetary system which beggars both."

When one of Watson's black supporters was threatened, Watson harbored him in his own house and called for help. Two thousand armed white farmers responded, keeping guard for two nights. After that, black support grew, and fear gripped Georgia's conservative rulers.

The Georgia election of 1892, won by the Democrats, was marked by violence. Armed gangs broke up Populist meetings, blacks who backed Watson were killed, and ballots were stolen. Black plantation hands were driven into town in wagonloads to vote the Democratic line under the watchful eyes of sheriffs.

"The worst thing that could happen," said a conservative, Henry Grady, "is that the white people of the South should stand in opposing factions, with the vast mass of ignorant and purchaseable Negro votes in between."

White Populists agreed. Furious over the black Democratic votes that provided the margins for their defeats, they wanted the black man removed from politics so that white men could dispute the issues without the fear of blacks holding the balance of power. The racism that had always been just below the surface of the Populist movement was now given free reign, and "farmers' candidates" throughout the South, including Tom Watson himself, became rabid racists.

In 1890, Mississippi held a convention to draft a new constitution that would result in disenfranchising blacks. The "Mississippi Plan" became the model for the South's attack on the black man's political rights. South Carolina adopted it in 1895, Louisiana in 1898, and other states soon after. By 1910, every southern state had effectively removed the black man from the balloting booth.

White politicians made no secret of their intentions. A Virginia convention leader declared: "Discrimination! Why that is precisely what we propose; that exactly is what this convention was elected for." And the president of the Louisiana convention, a former power in the White League, expressed his pleasure with the draft of the new constitution: "Doesn't it let the white man vote, and doesn't it stop the Negro from voting, and isn't that what we came here for?"

Another reason given for black disenfranchisement was, oddly enough, that it would ensure political "morality." "White men have gotten to cheating each other until we don't have honest elections," a former governor complained to the Alabama convention. A Mississippi delegate, admitting that "there has not been a full and fair count in Mississippi since 1875," declared that "no man can be in favor of perpetuating the election methods which have prevailed

. . . who is not a moral idiot." This strange argument—
that blacks must be punished to prevent whites from stealing their votes—made sense to the delegates to these conventions, all but a bare handful of whom were white.

The conventions used a variety of methods to achieve
their ends. The most common were literacy and property
qualifications for voters. Mississippi added an "understanding clause" that permitted illiterates to vote if they could
"understand" any section of the Constitution read to them.
This was a transparent device to let white illiterates vote
while barring blacks, since blacks were usually asked about
the most difficult parts of the Constitution. Even correct
answers from blacks would be disqualified by registrars.

The Louisiana convention invented the "grandfather
clause," which waived literacy and property qualifications
for anyone who was eligible to vote on January 1, 1867,
along with his sons and grandsons, another obvious loop-
hole that applied only to whites. The poll tax also became
a popular device, used by many states that never bothered
to write new constitutions. Payment of the tax was required
far in advance of elections, and it was accompanied by so
much red tape that blacks were sure to be its main victims.

The conventions did their dirty work well. Blacks who
somehow managed to escape the net cast by the new constitutions were prevented from voting by threats, fraud, and a
variety of tactics improvised by registrars who could not
find the voting lists or whose offices were mysteriously
closed for business upon the arrival of a black voter.

States that had primary elections—all important now
that the Populist rebellion was crushed and the Democratic
party was the only one with a chance of winning elections

—devised a "white primary" system to keep blacks out. A convention of Lauren County Democrats in South Carolina passed what became a model resolution: "No Negro shall vote in the next primary election who cannot prove by 5 responsible white Democrats that he voted with the Democracy for Hampton and the State ticket in 1876, and has been a Democrat ever since."

All of these laws and rules effectively took the black man's political rights from him. In 1897, for example, Louisiana had 130,000 registered black voters. By 1904, only a token 1,700 had the ballot. South Carolina's 92,000 black voters had shrunk to a mere 2,800 in 1898. And of 52,000 Mississippi blacks who voted in the election of 1876, there were only 3,500 by 1898.

Once the Negro had lost his political rights, it was an easy matter to take away his few remaining civil rights as well. The South began an orgy of oppression, the aim of which was to regulate the black man and "keep him in his place." State and local governments vied with each other to pass Jim Crow laws separating the races. Railroads were required to set aside special Jim Crow cars for blacks. Then separate streetcars were mandated. Jim Crow waiting rooms followed.

In the early years of the new century, the practice took firm hold. Some of the laws merely confirmed established social practices—hospitals and schools, for example, had always been segregated by custom—but the new laws became even more insane. Parks, theaters, libraries, and other public places either barred blacks or reserved special sections for them. The South was suddenly festooned with signs reading "Whites Only" or "Colored."

There were even Jim Crow Bibles for black witnesses in courts, and Jim Crow elevators in Atlanta office buildings. Two states separated school textbooks intended for use in the segregated schools, and Florida stipulated that the books be separated even in storage. A South Carolina law regulating textile factories not only forbade blacks and whites to work together in the same room, but also barred them from using the same staircases, pay windows, doorways, and even windows!

Militant blacks protested this growing oppression and organized boycotts against Jim Crow facilities in many cities. When Savannah, Georgia, passed a streetcar segregation law, the town's black newspaper declared: "Let us walk! walk! and save our nickels. . . . Do not trample on your pride by being 'jim crowed.' Walk!" Like the blacks of Montgomery, Alabama, half a century later, they did walk to support their civil rights. The streetcar company complained that the boycott cost it $50,000 in lost revenue, but the strike failed and Savannah joined the rest of the South in drawing the color line.

The elaborate rituals of the Jim Crow code were meant to give visible evidence of white supremacy, and the conservative white ruling classes used the Jim Crow device as much to keep poor whites in their place as to regulate blacks. Jim Crow gave the poor white a sense of privilege and superiority for merely being white. It kept him from realizing that the South's rulers were exploiting him also. The color line was drawn to feed the white worker's vanity, shield him from black competition, and destroy any hope of blacks and whites uniting in pursuit of their joint interests.

Lynching now became a custom in many parts of the South, and southern trees came to bear strange fruit—black bodies, victims of the mob. Hot, damp summer nights were torn by the cries of the victims; the scent of magnolia blossoms mingled with the smell of burning flesh. A look, a stare, a thoughtless word or deed, were enough to bring mob vengeance. Blacks suspected of crimes were taken from jails and lynched, often with the help of local policemen. Any "uppity" black, meaning anyone who saved money to buy a farm or tried to better his lot by taking schooling seriously, was fair game for the lynchers.

Rape of a white woman was the most serious offense of which a black man could be accused. Few blacks charged with the crime lived to see the inside of a court-room, and few of those lynched were ever guilty of the deed. Racial tensions would mount in a community, a woman would claim (often falsely) that she had been at-tacked, and a black man would soon be found hanging from a poplar, the victim of mob madness. One newspaper casually tucked into its back pages the following short item of news so common it hardly seemed worth more space: "Four Negroes were lynched in Grenada last week; also one at Oxford."

Northern opinion was silent in the face of the South's assault on the rights of black people. The abolitionist and Radical spirit was all but dead, and the general feeling among even "liberal" northerners was that the South had to work out its own problems. There was little sympathy for the black victims of racism. At this time the nation was emerging as an imperialist power, as the Spanish-American War of 1898 brought American power to the Caribbean and the Philippines. White northerners who dominated brown people abroad could hardly object to white southerners who dominated black people at home. "If the stronger and cleverer race," editorialized the influential *Atlantic Monthly,* "is free to impose its will upon 'new-caught sullen peoples' on the other side of the globe, why not in South Carolina and Mississippi?"

Powerful economic and political interests were also at work. Merchants and industrialists felt that any controversy over racial issues was bad for business. Republican presidents, from Rutherford B. Hayes onward, pursued a special "southern strategy." No longer the party of the Radicals, the Republicans had begun the struggle that continues to this day to break the "Solid South" away from the Democratic party. They sought to do this by forming alliances with southern businessmen who shared their desire for cheap labor and for protective tariffs on foreign goods.

Congress, too, abandoned the black man. It roundly defeated the only two major post-Reconstruction bills aimed at benefiting black people. One would have provided federal aid to education; the other would have installed federal supervisors to monitor southern elections, a measure similar to that finally enacted by the Voting Rights Bill of 1965.

But perhaps most damaging were the actions of the Supreme Court, which methodically dismantled the civil rights guarantees of Reconstruction. Law after law was struck down as unconstitutional by a court bent on stripping the black man of the protection of federal civil rights laws.

Finally in 1896, the Supreme Court reached the infamous decision in the case of *Plessy* v. *Ferguson,* upholding Jim Crow laws. Homer Plessy, who brought the suit, was a black man who, first-class ticket in hand, was ordered by a train conductor to the "colored coach" and was arrested for refusing. The High Court ruled that segregation was legal as long as accommodations were "separate but equal." In practice, of course, they were never "equal." The "colored coaches," for example, were dirty, drafty, and sometimes without rest rooms.

The Court's ruling sanctioned, and even encouraged, the spirit of Jim Crow. It provided legal cover for the traditional segregated schools, although they were obviously unequal. Southern states were spending $4.92 a year for the education of the average white pupil, $2.21 for the average black student. But not even surface equality could have made segregation less unequal. As the Court's lone dissenter, the former slaveholder John Marshall Harlan pointed out: "The arbitrary separation of citizens, on the basis of race . . . is a badge of servitude wholly inconsistent with the freedom and equality before the law established by the Constitution." It was not until 1954 that the notorious "separate but equal" doctrine was revoked.

Black people faced the dawn of a new century in the grip of oppression. The distinguished black novelist Charles W. Chestnutt sadly observed: "The rights of the Negroes are at a lower ebb than at any time during the thirty-five years of their freedom, and the race prejudice more intense and uncompromising."

12. Compromise and Protest

A "New South" was rising from the old; northern industry and money flowed into the region. The cream of Dixie's new aristocracy flocked to Atlanta in 1895 to see the fabulous Cotton States Exposition, a fair designed to attract even more northern investment. Speaker followed speaker, but one man captured the day. He was Booker T. Washington, principal of Tuskegee Institute, a small black industrial trade school nestled in Alabama's Black Belt. Looking out at the sea of white faces in the audience, he raised his hand high and spread his fingers wide. "In all things that are purely social, we can be as separate as the fingers," he said, and closing his hand into a fist, "yet one as the hand in all things essential to mutual progress." Speaking to black people he counseled: "Cast down your bucket where you are—cast it down in making friends in every manly way of the people of all races . . ."

Passive acceptance of the black man's lot was Washington's advice to his race. "It is at the bottom of life we must begin, and not at the top. Nor should we permit our grievances to overshadow our opportunities." He believed that racial progress would come from the sweat of honest labor.

"We shall prosper in proportion as we learn to dignify and glorify common labor and put brains and skill into the common occupations of life. . . . The agitation of questions of social equality is the extremest folly," he continued. "It is important and right that all the privileges of the law be ours, but it is vastly more important that we be prepared for the exercises of these privileges."

His white listeners were asked to "help and encourage" blacks and were promised that they would "be surrounded by the most patient, faithful, law-abiding, and unresentful people," who, "in our humble way . . . will stand by you with devotion." At this the crowd erupted into applause. Washington had touched a responsive chord. His humble tone, his pleading approach, his apparent acceptance of the social and economic order, his advice to his fellow blacks to resign themselves to their menial role— these were words that South's rulers and their northern allies wanted to hear.

Southern newspapers were ecstatic. "The most remarkable address delivered by a colored man in America," editorialized *The Atlanta Constitution*. A Charleston paper went about as far as it could in complimenting a black man: "His skin is colored but his head is sound and his heart is in the right place."

Washington's "Atlanta Compromise" thrust him into the position of unquestioned leader of America's blacks. For two decades, until his death in 1915, he was consulted by presidents on federal appointments, and northern philantropists gave him veto power over their spending for black causes. He controlled black opinion as well. He ruthlessly stripped his opponents of their jobs in schools dependent on donations from Washington's philanthropist friends or from jobs controlled by his political allies. He subsidized the black press, and it carried stories supporting him.

Booker T. Washington's humble public manner was misleading, a mask for an inner toughness. A contemporary described him as "wary and silent. He never expressed himself frankly or clearly until he knew exactly to whom he was talking and just what their wishes and desires were." This master of deception made southerners think he passively accepted their racism, but his private actions did not square with his public statements. Through liberal friends and black organizations dominated by his supporters, he organized attacks on segregation laws. He lobbied against passage of the new state constitutions that limited black political rights, and he secretly spent much of his own money in court fights against Jim Crow.

Washington was no quisling, no Uncle Tom, eager to sell out his own people. As he often said, "When your head is in the lion's mouth, use your hand to pet him." He strove to secure for black people at least a small measure of life, a breathing space, in a period of relentless oppression. His strategy was to make allies of rich northerners and moderate southerners and, through them, win the black man protection, education, and jobs. These men cooperated with Washington because, in the words of W. E. B. Du Bois, blacks "could become a strong labor force and properly guided they would restrain the unbridled demands of white labor, born of the Northern labor unions and now spreading in the South."

Washington shared with his wealthy supporters a faith in the materialistic spirit of the age. He believed that blacks had to gain a foothold in the economy and encouraged all-black businesses and all-black towns. In this, he was a forerunner of later separatists and nationalists who blended some of Washington's philosophy with the more militant statements of his critics.

Washington's strategy was short-term. He hoped for eventual equality, but even his limited goals were doomed to failure. He just never reckoned with the depth of white resistance, nor with the reluctance of his white supporters to oppose it. Many blacks who followed his advice and learned skilled trades or went into business found that, instead of winning the respect of their neighbors, they were singled out for greater oppression because their prosperity offended whites.

The South was scandalized when Booker T. Washington dined with President Theodore Roosevelt at the White House. "Now that Roosevelt has eaten with that nigger Washington," bellowed South Carolina's rabidly racist Senator Ben Tillman, "we shall have to kill a thousand niggers to get them back to their places."

In that era of lynch law and unbridled racism, black leaders could go one of two ways. They could seek a compromise, as Washington did, hoping to keep what little bit black people had and hope for better days to come, or they could organize militant protest to try and awaken the conscience of the nation, to stir the dying embers of the spirit that gave birth to abolitionism and Reconstruction. Some took that path, while a few followed both doctrines.

The most prominent of the militants who continued to support Washington was T. Thomas Fortune, outspoken editor of *The New York Age*. He once urged blacks who were put off first-class railroad coaches to defend their rights by arms: "One or two murders growing from this intolerable nuisance would break it up." Fortune also organized the Afro-American Council, which stressed self-help and racial pride.

Many of the militants, however, were violently anti-Washington. The Boston editor William Monroe Trotter addressed Booker T. Washington: "The colored people see and understand you; they know that you have marked their very freedom for destruction, and yet, they endure you almost without a murmur." In 1903 Trotter was arrested for his part in the "Boston Riot," actually a protest he led against Washington that prevented the Tuskegeean from finishing a speech. The audience went out of control when Trotter asked Washington, "Is the rope and the torch all the race is to get under your leadership?" Washington's most prominent critic, however, was W. E. B. Du Bois, and much of Negro history in the early years of this century was shaped by the rivalry of these two giants.

Booker T. Washington was born in slavery in about 1856, and by the time he was nine years old, he was a laborer in a salt mine. In his teens, he walked hundreds of miles to Hampton Institute in Virginia, where he worked his way through school. Becoming an educator in his own right, he founded Tuskegee Institute in 1881 as an industrial training school, modeled after Hampton. The Alabama school slowly became a reality as Washington worked alongside his students to put up its buildings and raise funds from local people.

Du Bois grew up in sharply contrasting circumstances. He was born to a middle-class Massachusetts family in 1868, twelve years after Washington was born. While the penniless young Booker was struggling and sacrificing to win an education, Du Bois was attending integrated public schools and went on to study at Fisk, at Berlin University, and at Harvard, where he became the first black man to receive a Ph.D. degree in history from the university. A distinguished scholar, Du Bois held a series of prestigious appointments and was an accomplished sociologist and historian, the author of several important books.

Each man's background was reflected in his philosophy of how blacks could best be helped. Washington was a believer in industrial education and in training blacks for skilled trades. Du Bois was known for his belief that salvation lay in developing an élite. "I believed," he wrote, "in the higher education of a Talented Tenth who through their knowledge of modern culture could guide the American Negro into a higher civilization." Without this, Du Bois argued, "the Negro would have to accept white leadership," and "such leadership could not always be trusted . . ."

Washington never had doubts about the spirit of rampant capitalism that characterized the age. Du Bois, on the other hand, recognized the economic forces that kept both white and black workers down and at each other's throats. He was sympathetic to the socialist ideas that were influencing urban intellectuals of the period. Although both men shared a belief in racial solidarity and self-help, Du Bois called for strengthening black institutions, and he insisted also upon complete equality and full participation of blacks in every aspect of American life. He scorned Washington's submissive attitudes, which "practically accepted the alleged inferiority of the Negro."

The inevitable split between the two men started in 1903 when Du Bois, who had at one time received an offer to teach at Tuskegee, published a slim volume of essays, *The Souls of Black Folk,* which included a respectful criticism of Washington. He soon felt the wrath of the "Tuskegee Machine," the term used to describe the pressures Washington and his followers brought upon their critics. Once in the open, their philosophical differences deepened and attracted public attention. Du Bois became a magnet for the anti-Bookerite faction, and by 1905 the rupture was irreparable.

In that year, Du Bois organized the Niagara Movement, named for the site of its first meeting, Niagara Falls. Washington's response was typical of the Tuskegee Machine in operation. "Telegraph newspapermen that you can absolutely trust," he instructed an aide, "to ignore the Niagara Movement."

But the outspoken new group could not easily be ignored. Unlike the Bookerites, it aggressively demanded black civil rights. As Du Bois said at the group's second annual meeting, which was held at Harpers Ferry, Virginia, "We will not be satisfied to take . . . less than our full manhood rights. We claim for ourselves every single right that belongs to a freeborn American, political, civil and social; and until we get these rights we will never cease to protest and assail the ears of America."

The small band of twenty-nine men who fathered the movement were soon joined by a few hundred—all distinguished representatives of Du Bois's "talented tenth." The group fought Jim Crow laws in the courts, held public protest meetings, and propagandized for civil rights. Eventually, Du Bois and most of the other members went over to the new National Association for the Advancement of Colored People, which in some ways was the successor to the Niagara Movement. It was destined to become the most influential civil rights organization in our history.

The NAACP had its beginnings in an article written by a white southern journalist, William English Walling, describing the horrors of a riot in Lincoln's hometown, Springfield, Illinois, in 1908. White mobs surged through the black ghetto in a frenzy of burning and looting. "Who realizes the seriousness of the situation," Walling asked, "and what large and powerful body of citizens is ready to come to their [blacks'] aid?"

A New York social worker, Mary White Ovington, was moved by this article to bring together citizens concerned about the racial crisis. A series of interracial meetings followed, shocking *The New York World* into exclaiming in a headline, "Whites and Negroes Mix at Conference." The NAACP grew out of these gatherings, and by 1910 it was a going organization. Du Bois, the only black among its leading officers, was editor of its magazine, *Crisis,* and chief propagandist.

The young organization mounted an attack on Jim Crow and lynching, through court actions and public protest. Some minor victories were capped by a major success in 1915, when the Supreme Court upheld an NAACP suit and ruled that the notorious "grandfather clause" that barred blacks from voting in some southern states was unconstitutional.

The National Urban League was born during this period, too. It was formed in New York in 1911 through the merger of three organizations that worked to improve economic and social conditions among the growing numbers of blacks in the cities. Supported by white philanthropists and staffed by professional social workers of both races, the league provided counseling, job training, and similar aid. It ran demonstration projects, such as day-care centers, to convince local authorities of the need for services in the ghetto. League agents met black migrants from the South at steamship piers and helped them adjust to the strange new world of the big city.

The early years of the twentieth century were a period of intense activity. Largely abandoned by white society, blacks banded together for self-help. Nurseries, clubs, settlement houses, orphanages, and similar institutions were founded. Women's clubs and churches were especially active in organizing welfare institutions. In Chicago, a black doctor, Daniel Hale Williams, founded Provident Hospital in 1891 to fill the needs of black doctors and patients, barred from white hospitals. Williams, who crowned his brilliant career by performing the first successful heart operation, also founded the Negro Medical Association with Booker T. Washington's aid in 1904.

Black businessmen were banding together as well. In 1900 Washington organized the Negro Business League. By 1907, there were 320 local chapters, which encouraged black capitalism and sponsored "buy black" campaigns. Black enterprise expanded quickly—but in segregated markets. Insurance companies, for example, grew out of fraternal benefit societies that had been formed precisely because white companies refused to insure blacks. By 1907 there were nearly seventy of these black-owned insurance companies. Spurred by segregation and by the Tuskegee belief in black capitalism, the 20,000 Negro businesses of 1900 had become 40,000 by 1914. This figure included 51 Negro-owned banks, 695 drugstores, and 25,000 retail stores.

Black workingmen, most of whom were farmers and farm laborers, were having a harder time. Some were reduced to a condition of semislavery known as "peonage" (from the Spanish word *peon,* a landless peasant), working to pay off debts charged to them by unscrupulous plantation owners.

Even skilled workers were often unable to get jobs or decent salaries because of union discrimination, as well as the refusal of many employers to hire blacks for "white men's work." In 1902, Du Bois found that forty-three major national unions barred blacks entirely while twenty-seven others had only token numbers. Only forty thousand Negro workers were among the more than one million members of the American Federation of Labor, and most of them belonged to the miners' union. Such discrimination was not new. As far back as 1869, black workers had formed the National Negro Labor Congress because white unions would not admit them.

Employers often exploited the discord between white and black workers, importing black laborers to break strikes called by white unions. In 1896, Alabama blacks read handbills with headlines such as this one: "Wanted! colored coal-miners for Weir City, Kan. district, the paradise for colored people. Get ready and go to the land of promise." The circular never mentioned that the black miners were being hired to scab. When the first arrived at Weir City, they were met by the white miners who explained the situation. Most of the blacks refused to scab and returned home.

At other times, blacks were met by gunfire as strikers vainly sought to protect their jobs. Often black workers were ignorant of the meaning of strikes and simply went to work, only to be fired as soon as the strike was settled. White immigrant groups were also often used as strikebreakers, but blacks were more visible because of their color and were also more likely to take any opportunity to enter trades from which they had been barred by white employers and unions.

The use of black strikebreakers, especially in major labor crises, such as the Chicago stockyards strike of 1904 and the Chicago teamsters strike of 1905, reinforced union prejudice against blacks. In its first years, the American Federation of Labor seemed favorable to organizing black workers, stating that "the working people must unite and organize, irrespective of creed, color, sex, nationality, or politics." But the AFL soon realized that any attempt to force this stand on member unions that followed Jim Crow policies would split the labor movement. As a substitute for equality, the AFL chartered all-black locals under the control of Jim Crow parent unions. The black locals had little bargaining power. In reality, the growing American labor movement had decisively closed its doors to the black workingman.

Blacks, however, overcame these and other obstacles as talented individuals climbed over the color barrier. Black inventors supplied a burgeoning industrial society with tools for progress. Granville T. Woods, for example, became known as the "Black Edison" for his many discoveries, including one that made possible communication between moving trains, and Lewis Latimer improved Edison's electric light bulb by inventing a socket similar to the one we use today.

Other black men followed in the footsteps of the black explorers who left their mark on an earlier age. Matthew Henson was a key member of Admiral Robert E. Peary's North Pole expedition in 1909 and was actually the first man to locate the pole.

In an earlier period, other black adventurers made their way west, where they were cowboys and rodeo stars. Somehow the cowboys in western films always manage to be white, but that has more to do with Hollywood's racism than with history. Black cowboys like Nat Love—better known as Deadwood Dick—were a major part of the western scene, fighting rustlers, driving cattle north from Texas, and rubbing elbows with almost legendary figures like Bat Masterson and Buffalo Bill. And when the cavalry came to the rescue, chances were they were black. Two black cavalry regiments were sent west after the Civil War. Black troops captured Geronimo, fought against Apache warriors, and trapped Billy the Kid.

Black troops fought in the Spanish-American War of 1898. Thirty black sailors went down with the battleship *Maine* when she sank in Havana harbor, the incident that led to the war. In the famous Battle of San Juan Hill, the black cavalry knocked out a Spanish fort, enabling Teddy Roosevelt's Rough Riders to storm up the hill and win glory. "If it had not been for the Negro cavalry," one white southern officer said, "the Rough Riders would have been exterminated."

In 1906, Roosevelt repaid the favor with an act that shocked blacks all over the country. In Brownsville, Texas, a white officer had fired into a mob and started a riot. Some said that it involved black troops of the Twenty-fifth Regiment, an outfit that had seen service in Cuba during the Spanish-American War. President Roosevelt believed reports that the black troopers had shot up the town (although it was the black ghetto that was burned) and dishonorably discharged three whole companies of the regiment. A later investigation cleared the men, but the damage had been done.

Another riot, still more bloody, took place in Atlanta a month later. White mobs, inflamed by newspaper headlines falsely charging a black crime wave, invaded black neighborhoods, burning and shooting. The riots ended when blacks armed themselves and fought off the rioters, one of the most forceful signs of blacks' determination to defend themselves against racist violence.

Such incidents were a reflection of the deep-rooted racism of the period. Books appeared with titles such as *The Negro: A Menace to Civilization* and *The Negro a Beast*. Popular songs and films held blacks up to ridicule, and scientific evidence was twisted or fabricated to "prove" blacks inferior. A South African visitor was amazed at how closely American racism resembled that of his own country. "How often the very conditions I had left were reproduced before my eyes," he exclaimed. "Thousands of miles melted away and Africa was before me."

By the 1890s there was little doubt that the dream of freedom had turned into a nightmare of oppression. Growing numbers of southern blacks decided to leave the South.

As early as 1879, some black people had been swept by "Kansas fever." Some forty thousand from the Deep South fled to the Midwest, most of them to Kansas, where they believed they would get land and high wages. Railroad companies, who stood to make money on their fares, circulated brightly colored posters depicting black farmers sitting before tables heaped with food, while beyond the windows sleek cattle grazed and rich crops ripened in the fields. The reality was quite different. Barefoot farm laborers in light cotton shirts stepped off the Mississippi steamers to find snow piled high on the freezing piers. Kansans, at first hospitable, turned against the newcomers as their numbers increased and with it their need for help. At the same time, southern planters, furious at the prospect of losing their cheap labor supply, tried to stop fieldhands from leaving. One group, led by a former Confederate general, blockaded river landings on the Mississippi, threatening to sink any boat carrying blacks north.

"Kansas fever" died out, but other migration movements replaced it. There was one aimed at making Oklahoma a separate black state, and twenty-five all-black towns were settled. But that movement, too, could not overcome the hostility of whites and native Indian tribes. The idea of all-black towns spread, however, and many were established from New Jersey to California. Two of the most prominent, both aided by Booker T. Washington, were Mound Bayou, Mississippi, and Boley, Oklahoma. Both survive to this day.

Back-to-Africa movements also drew new strength during the 1880s and 1890s when some Liberia-bound ships actually carried blacks out of the Southland. The most prominent leader in the new African colonization efforts was Bishop Henry McNeal Turner, an outspoken Georgian who had lived and traveled in Africa. "We were born here," Turner wrote, "raised here, fought, bled, and died here, and have a thousand times more right here than hundreds of thousands of those who help to snub, proscribe and persecute us, and that is one of the reasons I almost despise the land of my birth." Turner dreamed of a powerful African state that would give blacks a national identity and self-respect like other ethnic groups. "Till we have black men in the seat of power, respected, feared, hated and reverenced," he said, "our young men will never rise for the reason they will never look up."

Turner's nationalism, like that of Marcus Garvey a generation later, appealed to many poor blacks but earned the enmity of most black leaders. While Africa was far away, lost in a mist of myth, the North was near, and it, too, promised relief from the relentless oppression and exploitation of the South.

13. The Great Migration

"I am in the darkness of the south and i am trying my best to get out do you no where about i can get a job in new york . . . o please help me to get out of this low down country i am counted no more thin a dog help me please help me . . ." Letters like this one poured into the offices of the Chicago *Defender,* a black newspaper, around the year 1915 as poor, semiliterate farmhands wrote appealing for work and help to come north.

In Birmingham, Alabama, in Jackson, Mississippi, in Memphis, Tennessee, and other towns of the South, black men, their work clothes still bearing the stains of field labor, boarded trains bound for the North. Their hands clutched cardboard suitcases in which all their worldly possessions were locked. And in their hearts was hope—for a new chance in life, away from the threat of lynch mobs, away from dawn-to-dusk plantation labor.

Special trains pulled out of southern railway depots. On their sides were chalked slogans: "Farewell—We're Good and Gone," "Bound for the Promised Land," and

"Bound to the Land of Hope." A poem in the *Defender* described the exodus:

> "I've watched the trains as they disappeared
> Behind the clouds of smoke,
> Carrying the crowds of working men
> To the land of Hope."

The *Defender* was a carrier of the "northern fever" that swept the black South in the years before America's entry into World War I. Its pages told of high wages and steady work in northern factories, of a free atmosphere, and of fairer treatment. The paper's glowing reports of conditions in the North were reinforced by letters from new migrants who wrote home describing the excitement of the city and the plentiful opportunities for black people. Sometimes the letters included a new five- or ten-dollar bill— proof that black people could prosper in the North. Labor agents helped spread word of factory openings in the North and aided prospective migrants in getting train tickets. The trickle became a flood; the tide of black discontent whirled masses of workers northward.

The southern planters and businessmen were furious. Their cheap labor supply was leaving, lured by "outside agitators." Some places barred the *Defender,* punishing blacks who were found with a copy of the paper, much as persons found with abolitionist papers of an earlier day had been punished. Several cities passed laws against the northern labor recruiters. The Macon, Georgia, city council set a fee of $25,000 for a license to recruit labor, adding the requirement that an agent had first to be recommended by ten ministers and twenty-five local businessmen. Montgomery,

Alabama, went further; it set stiff fines and jail terms for anyone guilty of "enticing, persuading, or influencing" workers to leave town.

Such limitations on a black man's freedom were a major reason for the move northward, as were the conditions of semislavery on the plantations. Economic motives, however, played the biggest role. To laborers who worked twelve-hour days for a dollar or less, northern factory jobs at $4 or $5 a day seemed like paradise.

The boll weevil played a part in the migration, too. The small black bug made its home in cotton plants, its young feeding on the growing cotton fibers. It started in Mexico and swept across Texas, spreading devastation and causing an economic depression throughout the lower South. Farm laborers were thrown out of work or had their wages lowered. By 1916, the boll weevil had sped through Georgia, and by 1919, it had ruined South Carolina's cotton crop. Blacks sang:

> "The merchant got half the cotton,
> the boll weevil got the res'.
> Didn't leave the farmer's wife
> but one old cotton dress
> and it's full of holes, it's full of holes."

A million blacks moved north between 1910 and 1924. Black people were well on their way to becoming city dwellers. Back in 1890, only one out of five blacks lived in cities, but by 1920, one out of three were urbanites. In some of the big northern industrial centers, the northward migration was especially dramatic. Detroit, for example, had less than six thousand blacks in 1910, but the new auto industry opened up job opportunities, and by 1920, there were over forty thousand blacks in the city. Booming industrial plants of the North needed workers, and with immigration slowed to a trickle by restrictive immigration laws after the war, there were jobs aplenty for black newcomers.

City life was a strange experience for them. Agencies such as the Urban League helped them find jobs and adjust to new ways. Churches and social and fraternal groups did their share, too. The *Defender* not only urged blacks to come north, but also gave them tips about how to act once they arrived.

"Quit calling the foreman 'boss,' " the newspaper advised. "Also captain, general, and major. We call people up here Mister." It urged workers to "appear on the streetcars and in public places in clean, decent clothes," and complained of "loafers hanging around the poolrooms" and gambling and drinking. The *Defender* warned against "scheming preachers and labor agents," and other city hustlers who separated the newcomers from their wages. The paper also cautioned against southern sheriffs who traveled to northern cities like the slave catchers of olden times. They would come up to an unsuspecting migrant and try to arrest him for "spitting on the sidewalk" back home or for debts "owed" to his plantation boss.

Most of the migrants found more freedom, work, and relatively higher wages in the North, but a thick wall of prejudice and discrimination separated the races. This was especially marked in housing, as blacks were forced into ghettos and charged higher rents for slum quarters. As new migrants arrived, the borders of the black community pushed outward, creating large all-black districts.

The growth of black Harlem is an example. At the turn of the century, Harlem was a white middle-class neighborhood. Large, high-ceilinged apartments in elegant buildings made it one of New York's more desirable neighborhoods, but there were many vacancies due to overbuilding. A black real-estate man talked the white owners of buildings on 134th Street into renting long-vacant apartments to blacks. He assured the owners that black tenants would pay higher rents to escape their downtown slums. Many whites objected, however, and fought to bar blacks from buildings in Harlem. Black real-estate men countered by buying buildings themselves and replacing white tenants with blacks. Soon, black churches were buying property in Harlem and renting to blacks.

As the small black colony expanded, whites began to leave the neighborhood. Many landlords sold to blacks or relaxed their own ban on blacks. Notices started to appear on tenement walls:

NOTICE
We have endeavored for some time to
avoid turning over this house to
colored tenants, but as a result of . . .
rapid changes in conditions . . . this
issue has been forced upon us.

Harlem, which had only 300 black families in 1903, rapidly became the largest black ghetto in the country. Between 1920 and 1930, about 120,000 whites left the area, and 90,000 Negroes replaced them. By 1930, Harlem was home to 165,000 black people.

The black influx was often resisted violently. Property owners in Chicago, for example, used threats and bombings to try to scare blacks out of moving into their neighborhoods. Black tenants in one building received notices that read: "We are going to Blow these FLATS TO HELL and if you don't want to go with them you had better move at once." These were not idle threats. Between 1917 and 1921, there were five such bombings in Chicago. A local newspaper wrote, with more heat than logic, that "every colored man who moves into Hyde Park . . . is making war on the white man. Consequently he is not entitled to any consideration and forfeits his right to be employed by the white man."

White property owners also resorted to agreements not to sell their homes to blacks. These were written into contracts and deeds, preventing resale of homes to blacks. Such tactics led to population increases in the black neighborhoods as more people were squeezed into already overcrowded space. Municipal services to black areas declined, and the ghetto often became a slum.

There were job hardships, too. Working in a factory was better than chopping cotton, but many jobs were closed to black workers. One employer candidly admitted that he hired blacks only because of the labor shortage and as soon as the situation changed, no more would be employed. Black workers were the last hired and the first fired. They were relegated to the lowest paying jobs with the least status, and they almost never rose to positions of authority over white men.

Jim Crow even reached its tentacles into the ranks of the federal government. Black job applicants were screened out, and President Woodrow Wilson allowed major government departments to institute segregation. Blacks were forced to use Jim Crow lavatories and lunchrooms and were separated from their white co-workers in government offices.

Southern mobs still went on lynching parties. In 1916, more than one black a week was lynched, and one man in Waco, Texas, was burned alive before a chanting, screaming mob of ten thousand, who fought for his remains as souvenirs. The next year, in Memphis, fifteen thousand people took part in a similar atrocity. Thus, when the country entered World War I in 1917, the national battle cry, "Make the World Safe for Democracy," rang ironically in black ears.

A letter written to a New York newspaper asked: "Should a black man shoulder a gun and go to war and fight for this country which denies him the rights of citizenship, under a flag which offers him no protection, strips him of his manhood by enacting laws which keep him from the ballot box, disenfranchised, segregated, discriminated against, lynched, burned at the stake, Jim-Crowed and disarmed. If he fights and fight he must, for what does he fight?"

Negro leadership, however, saw the war as an opportunity for blacks to win equal rights. "If we fight," wrote Du Bois, "we'll learn the fighting game and cease to be so 'asily lynched.' If we don't fight, we'll learn the more lucrative trades and cease to be so easily robbed and exploited." In an editorial in the NAACP's *Crisis,* Du Bois called on blacks to "forget our special grievances and close ranks shoulder to shoulder with our fellow citizens," and to make sacrifices "gladly and willingly with our eyes lifted to the hills." In the end, though, the NAACP, which was committed to complete integration, had to accept not only the indignity of all black army units, but it also had to fight for segregated officer-training camps because that was the only way blacks could win commissions.

Most training camps were in the South, and southern attitudes toward black soldiers were reflected in the fear expressed by a southern senator that "millions of Negroes . . . will be armed. I know of no greater menace to the South than this." The commander of the all-black Ninety-second Division told his men to toe the line and observe Jim Crow customs. "White men made the Division," he warned, "and they can break it just as easily if it becomes a troublemaker."

Army posts themselves were Jim Crowed, and black troopers were barred from some buildings, recreational facilities, and even prayer meetings. Tensions mounted in the camps and sometimes burst into violence. Clashes between black soldiers and white civilians in Houston in 1917 resulted in a mass murder trial, with thirteen soldiers hanged and forty-one sentenced to life imprisonment.

Only a few months before that, the industrial town of East St. Louis, Illinois, had erupted in riots that claimed the lives of 125 blacks, while hundreds more were injured and thousands fled the town. In Harlem, 15,000 blacks marched down Fifth Avenue in silent protest against the riot and against mistreatment of black soldiers bearing signs that read: "Mr. President, Why Not Make America Safe for Democracy?" and "Treat Us So That We May Love Our Country."

Official Army policy remained bitterly antiblack, at

times infecting America's allies. A secret French directive laid down ground rules for the treatment of black soldiers so as not to offend American racial sensibilities. "We must prevent . . . intimacy between French officers and black officers," the directive stated. "We must not eat with them, must not shake hands or seek to talk or meet with them outside of the requirements of military service." The command cautioned, "We must not commend too highly the black American troops, particularly in the presence of [white] Americans." And the French officers were warned to "make a point of keeping the native population from spoiling the Negroes. White Americans become incensed at any public expression of intimacy between white women and black men . . ." The document probably came from American headquarters, although it bore the signatures of two French officers. The French War Department eventually burned all the copies it could get its hands on.

The Army did not trust black soldiers to fight. Three-fourths of the 200,000 blacks shipped to Europe were in labor battalions, unloading ships, carrying supplies, and doing the heavy, dirty work behind the lines. But several units saw action and performed with distinction—despite poor training, hostile higher officers, and the low morale brought about by discrimination. The 369th Regiment spent 191 days at the front, longer than any other unit. The French, to whom black combat units were assigned, awarded the coveted Croix de Guerre to three all-black units and, in 1918, asked American headquarters for all the black troops it could send to fight in the last big offensives of the war.

All too often, though, the heroism of black soldiers

met scorn from their white fellow-Americans. A Milwaukee editor wrote of black units that spearheaded the Argonne offensive, "Those two American colored regiments fought well, and it calls for special recognition. Is there no way of getting a cargo of watermelons over there?"

American officers chose not to remember the exploits of black fighting men, concentrating instead on the supposed shortcomings of one black unit, the 368th Infantry Regiment, which weakened in the battle of the Argonne Forest. Its junior black officers were blamed for the unit's poor performance, although the badly trained group never got artillery support for its advance and was hampered by bad leadership from white officers higher in the chain of command. Later General C. C. Ballou, in charge of the division of which the 368th was a part, was to say: "It was my misfortune to be handicapped by many white officers who were rabidly hostile to the idea of a colored officer, and who continually conveyed misinformation to the staff of the superior units, and generally created much trouble and discontent. Such men will never give the Negro the square deal that is his due."

Black men, nevertheless, came home from the battlefront with new dignity and pride. They marched in victory parades with flags flying and hearts pounding. "Make way for Democracy!" Du Bois exulted. "We saved it in France, and by the Great Jehovah, we will save it in the United States of America, or know the reason why."

The reason why was soon apparent. During the "red summer" of 1919, the nation was swept by bloody anti-black riots in twenty-six cities. Washington, D.C., itself was in the hands of a white mob, which, aided by bigoted police, attacked blacks. A newspaper scare campaign that daily featured banner headlines about a supposed black crime wave led to the outburst, which took federal troops to quell. Blacks engaged in organized resistance to the rioters, fighting off white invaders of black neighborhoods with shotguns.

Perhaps the biggest riot broke out in Chicago, where tensions over housing segregation reached the breaking point. One hot Sunday afternoon in July, a young black swam past the invisible line that divided a beach informally segregated into white and black sections. White bathers threw stones at him and he drowned. When a white policeman refused to arrest the stone-throwers, fighting broke out. Within hours, it had turned into a city-wide race riot.

Whites roamed the streets, picking blacks off streetcars and beating them. Shootings and knifings spread. The police seemed powerless to defend blacks and often joined in the beatings. Blacks defended themselves, beating and shooting whites who strayed into the ghetto. After thirty-eight people had been killed and hundreds injured, most of them black, the militia was called out to restore order. A special commission created to study the causes of the riot found, as similar commissions were to do in the 1960s, that the rampant bigotry and lack of opportunities for blacks were the main causes of the social tensions that led to bloodshed. Only equal rights and opportunities, the commission concluded, could bring racial peace.

The bloodshed in the North made southerners jubilant. Labor agents were sent to Chicago to recruit blacks to come back to work on the plantations. One such agent, who held a meeting of black workmen, described the marvelous harmony in the South and the high wages he would pay for sawing logs. "How many of you wish to go?" he asked. Silence. Finally one man said, "I tell you what you do—you send the logs up to Chicago, and we'll saw them here."

In September the true face of the South was seen in another riot, in Arkansas. A group of black sharecroppers in Phillips County met in a church to form a union. White men, including a deputy sheriff, surrounded the church and riddled it with bullets. When their fire was returned, the whites panicked and claimed the blacks were plotting a revolution. A bloody week followed. White vigilantes roamed the county, killed fifty or sixty blacks, and herded hundreds more to the county seat for trial and "investigation." Torture was used to extract "confessions," and twelve black farmers were sentenced to death while sixty-seven others went to prison. The NAACP fought the verdict and won a reversal from the Supreme Court because the black men had not been given a fair trial.

The Ku Klux Klan also was riding again. Interest in the Klan was stirred by a 1915 movie, *Birth of a Nation*. The film, made by the southerner, D. W. Griffith, from a novel by a leading racist propagandist of the time, Thomas Dixon, portrayed the old Klan of Reconstruction days in a very favorable light. Its romantic view of the Old South as a land of gentleness and magnolia-scented graciousness that was spoiled by the evil machinations of mulatto politicians, money-grubbing schemers, and the like appealed to audiences of the day. Griffith's noble Klansmen, avenging the rape and pillage of the evil blacks and northerners, were like brave medieval heroes, riding into the night in pursuit of justice and glory. Griffith was a master director, and he gave his tale a sweep and a power never before seen on the screen, influencing many in the audience to accept his twisted account of history. NAACP pickets paraded in front of theaters that showed the film, but when word got out that President Wilson and Edward White, Chief Justice of the United States, strongly recommended the movie, its success was assured.

In the 1920s the Klan was a political power to be reckoned with. It controlled many local governments and backed candidates for statewide offices even in northern states like Indiana and Oregon. In 1925, Klansmen in hoods and robes marched for hours in a parade past the White House.

The high hopes of black people that their loyalty and sacrifices in the war would win the rights other citizens took for granted were dashed. Black soldiers returned home to find the mobs, the lynch parties, and the poverty-stricken conditions they had left behind. A new bitterness grew, and faith in American society faded. From this bitterness rose a magnetic leader who preached black pride and black power —Marcus Garvey.

Garvey was a man with a mission. Inspired by the example and the thoughts of Booker T. Washington, he believed black people would have to help themselves if they were to achieve greatness. Echoing Washington, he said, "No man will do as much for you as you will do for yourself."

Born on the island of Jamaica, Garvey came to New York in 1916, and by 1921, his Universal Negro Improvement Association had a membership estimated at four million. He was scorned by the established black leadership and educated blacks, but Garvey touched the raw nerve of black nationalism among the masses, and they flocked to his banner. A master propagandist, he held rallies that sang the association's hymn, "Ethiopia, Thou Land of Our Fathers." His blue and red-clad African Legion paraded through Harlem's streets, followed by the white-uniformed Black Cross Nurses. The Universal Negro Improvement Association tricolor—black for skin color, green for hope, and red for blood—waved in the breeze.

Garvey founded the Black Star Line, a shipping company, and his organization ran a chain of grocery stores, a laundry, a publishing house, and other businesses. Yet, Garvey's nationalism transcended America's borders. "If Europe is for the European, then Africa shall be for the black peoples of the World," he proclaimed. "The other races have countries of their own and it is time for the 400 million Negroes to claim Africa for themselves." Garvey's call for a Black Republic of Africa and his attempt to build a black business empire were basic parts of a program of racial solidarity and pride. "I am the equal of any white man," he declared, "and I want you to feel the same way." Garvey asked: "Where is the black man's government? Where is his king and his kingdom? Where is his president, his country, and his ambassador, his army, his navy, his men of big affairs? I could not find them. I declared: I will help make them!"

His violent attacks on established black leaders and on light-skinned blacks earned their hatred. Many looked upon his schemes as impractical or worse. After Garvey met with the leader of the Ku Klux Klan, Du Bois blasted him: "Marcus Garvey is, without doubt, the most dangerous enemy of the Negro race in America and the world. He is either a lunatic or a traitor." Another critic described the self-proclaimed "Provisional President of Africa" as "squat stocky, fat, and sleek with protruding jaws and heavy jowls; small, bright, piglike eyes, and rather full doglike face. Boastful, egotistic, tyrannical, intolerant . . . and so forth."

Garvey's downfall came when his Black Star Line sailed into troubled financial waters and he was convicted of mail fraud. He disappeared behind prison walls in 1925, and two years later he was deported. Garvey's moment in the sun was fleeting. His schemes for a return to Africa and for a black business empire lay in ruins.

Garvey's short-lived movement was perhaps the largest mass movement of black people in history. His charismatic leadership rallied millions to his cause, but once he was removed from the scene, it melted away. His hard-core supporters continued to preach black nationalism, and Garvey's influence continues to this day as such groups as CORE openly describe themselves as "Garveyites." But Garvey's program was removed from the daily concerns of the black masses, and his own character deficiencies and administrative failings contributed to the inevitable decline of his movement. Garvey offered emotional release from the burdens of being black in a nation that still preached white supremacy, but he did not offer a reasonably realistic program that would lead to black progress, nor did his constant attacks on black leaders and on lighter-skinned black people help to bring about the unity blacks so desperately needed.

At the same time that Garvey's brand of extreme nationalism was making itself felt in the tenements and streets of the black ghettos, a nationalistic "cultural revolution" gripped black artists and writers. Black intellectuals preached racial solidarity and pride. They turned to the rich fabric of black experience to create poetry and novels that expressed the mood and the hopes of their people. Their credo might have been taken from this passage from Jessie Fauset's novel, *Plum Bun:*

"Those of us who have forged forward are not able as yet to go our separate ways from the unwashed, untutored herd. We must still look back and render service to our less fortunate, weaker brethren. And the first step toward making this a workable attitude is the acquisition not so much of a racial love as a racial pride. A pride that enables us to find our own beautiful and praiseworthy, an intense chauvinism that is content with its own types, that finds completeness within its own group, that loves its own as the French love their country."

The ghetto was filled with the music that gave the twenties the name of "the jazz age." The blues music that evolved from slave chants and gospel songs blended with European instruments and elements at about the turn of the century to become a new music—jazz. It was the black man's music; it resounded through the back streets of New Orleans, the Kansas City ghetto, the South Side of Chicago, and the asphalt streets of Harlem. Enthusiastic audiences stomped in time to Louis Armstrong's trumpet virtuosity, laughed at the sly songs of Bessie Smith, and wept as she, Ma Rainey, and others sang of unrequited love, violent death, and poverty.

White devotees made the trek uptown to hear the black
man's music; for a while, the flourishing ghetto-based culture made inroads among whites who collected African art,
read black writers, and listened to jazz. Some Harlem jazz
clubs, however, were rigidly segregated, and all-white audiences filled the Cotton Club to hear the genius of Duke Ellington and his orchestra and to watch the beautiful black,
brown, and beige chorus girls, but no black patrons were
admitted.

The black artists of what became known as the Harlem Renaissance gathered at the Schomburg Library, at
A'Lelia Walker's Harlem mansion, Dark Towers, and at
the homes of white patrons of the arts in Greenwich Village. They published their works in the NAACP's magazine, *Crisis,* the Urban League's *Opportunity,* and a host
of other small magazines of the time. Bards such as Langston Hughes sang the glories of Harlem life, fusing jazz
rhythms with poetry, while militants like Claude McKay
wrote battle cries for the war against oppression:

"If we must die, let it not be like hogs
  Hunted and penned in an inglorious spot,
  While round us bark the mad and hungry dogs,
  Making their mock at our accursed lot.
  If we must die, O let us nobly die,
  So that our precious blood may not be shed
  In vain; then even the monsters we defy
  Shall be constrained to honor us though dead!
  O kinsmen! we must meet the common foe!
  Though far outnumbered let us show us brave,
  And for their thousand blows deal one deathblow!

What though before us lies the open grave?
Like men we'll face the murderous, cowardly pack,
Pressed to the wall, dying, but fighting back!"

By the time Alain Locke published his anthology of Harlem Renaissance writers, *The New Negro,* in 1925, black writers were solidly established as the cultural vanguard of a new awakening in the ghetto and as a force in the cultural life of the nation.

Harder times were, however, in store for blacks—and whites. As Locke was to write, "The rosy enthusiasms and hopes of 1925 were . . . cruelly deceptive mirages." Racial pride was no bulwark against economic depression, and when the country slid down the precipice of falling wages and unemployment, the "new Negro" slid with it. As Locke admitted, "There is no cure or saving magic in poetry and art for . . . precarious marginal employment, high mortality rates, civic neglect."

14. Depression and War

"The Depression brought everybody down a peg or two," wrote Langston Hughes, "and the Negroes had but few pegs to fall."

The high-flying twenties ended in economic ruin. Hard times were here, and the black man had the hardest time of all. Black sharecroppers existed on semistarvation diets. In the cities, men roamed the streets aimlessly, their jobs gone, their savings lost in banks that went out of business, and in their pockets eviction notices. Women assembled in what were called slave markets to hire themselves out for domestic work at fifteen and twenty cents an hour. In the depth of the Depression, one out of every four black workers was unemployed. Nearly one in five was forced onto the relief rolls, and in some cities, the toll was much higher.

Hope revived when Franklin D. Roosevelt became President in 1933 and launched his New Deal. Dozens of new programs were set up to get the economy moving again and to relieve the misery that gripped the nation. The New Deal's impact was felt in every corner of the land, and black people benefited from its programs, especially in the North. Blacks got jobs on federal work relief programs.

Young people in the ghetto entered the Civilian Conservation Corps, a program that set them to work on reforestation, prevention of soil erosion, and similar conservation projects and paid their families a monthly stipend. Black families found homes in subsidized federal housing projects. While the federal housing program was often segregated, it still provided more than forty thousand decent low-cost homes for blacks, a third of the total building undertaken.

Although many New Deal programs relieved black poverty, they were administered by local authorities in a discriminatory way. Wages for blacks were often pegged lower than wages for whites, and federal farm programs, especially, aided white landowners at the expense of their black tenant-farmers. Cash benefits from the government enabled farmers to mechanize, throwing black sharecroppers and tenants out of work. The government also paid farmers money to supplement the low prices their products fetched on the open market, but in many cases unscrupulous landlords would not give their black tenants their rightful share of the money.

Despite strong pressures from Washington, southern authorities tried to keep blacks out of federal programs. Georgia officials attempted to bar black youths from the Civilian Conservation Corps, protesting that "few Negro families . . . need an income as great as $25 a month in cash"—the amount paid to families of workers.

Blacks, however, benefited more from the New Deal than from any previous administration in American history. They were appointed to high office, and key administration figures, including Mrs. Eleanor Roosevelt, were strong battlers for equal rights. A close friend of Mrs. Roosevelt was the black educator, Mary McLeod Bethune, who in 1935 founded the National Council of Negro Women to enlist black women in the civil rights cause. Mrs. Bethune was one of the highest ranking blacks in government, holding a high executive post in the National Youth Administration, and her friendship with the First Lady made her among the most influential blacks of the New Deal era.

When, in 1939, the Daughters of the American Revolution refused to allow the great black contralto Marian Anderson to sing in Constitution Hall in Washington, Mrs. Roosevelt arranged for the concert to be held at the Lincoln Memorial, where 75,000 people gathered at the feet of the Great Emancipator, dealing a symbolic blow to racism. Efforts such as those made by Mrs. Roosevelt were invaluable, but the brunt of the battle was borne by blacks themselves.

As the Depression deepened, even "Negro jobs" —those of porters, janitors, elevator men—went to unemployed whites. In the early thirties, black pickets bearing BUY BLACK signs marched in front of ghetto stores that did not hire blacks. "Buy black" campaigns in Washington, Chicago, New York, and other cities were often successful, and black workers—many of them unemployed college graduates—were hired as store clerks or typists.

Whatever advances were made under the New Deal, the Depression kept racial tension smoldering throughout the country. In 1935, a riot was kindled in Harlem by a rumor that a white shopkeeper had killed a young black. The rumor was not true, but thousands of blacks swept through the main streets shattering store windows and taking out their frustrations at discrimination by large-scale looting.

The growing despair among blacks reached into the ranks of the NAACP, where the long-time foe of segregation, W. E. B. Du Bois, came out in favor of voluntary segregation in the form of all-black businesses and all-black "groups of communities and farms." Du Bois argued that racist barriers to integration were far too high to be scaled in the near future and that blacks had to build "beneath them a strong foundation for self-support and social uplift." This, he said, would bring economic security and strengthen black people in an assault on the color line.

His critics, including NAACP leaders such as Walter White and James Weldon Johnson, disagreed. In a public argument like the debates in the 1960s between black power advocates and integrationists, they held fast to the belief that self-segregation could not be temporary. "Voluntary isolation would be a permanent secondary status," declared Johnson, and White threw Du Bois's own words back at him: "Just as soon as they get a group of black folk segregated, they use it as a point of attack and discrimination." The conflict resulted in Du Bois's leaving the NAACP, and the organization continued to devote its energies to attacks on the color line and court fights against Jim Crow laws.

In 1931, world attention was focused on a case of "legal lynching" in the South. Nine black teen-agers were pulled off a freight train near Scottsboro, Alabama, and charged with raping two white girls. Within two weeks southern "justice" sentenced all but the youngest to die in the electric chair. The case was appealed, and although the girls were revealed to be prostitutes and one of them admitted she had lied, the black defendants were repeatedly convicted. Finally, in 1935, the Supreme Court set aside the verdict in a landmark decision based on the fact that blacks were excluded from juries. Although their lives were saved, the Scottsboro Boys, as they had become known to the world, still served long jail terms. It was not until 1950 that the last of the nine was freed.

The Communist party was among the most prominent defenders of the Scottsboro Boys, and it hoped to use its role in the case to build black support. But it misjudged black aspirations. The party's policy was separatist; it advocated carving a separate black state out of the southern Black Belt, an aim shared by very few blacks. The Depression-ridden thirties, however, saw many people angered by mass poverty and injustice, and Communists often formed "popular front" organizations with them.

One such group was the National Negro Congress, founded in 1936. Its first president was perhaps the most dynamic black leader of the period, A. Philip Randolph. Randolph had been a militant leader since pre-World War I days, when he edited a fiery magazine called *The Messenger* with Chandler Owen. He put his belief in militant labor action into practice in the 1920s when he formed the Brotherhood of Sleeping Car Porters. The union was the first successful effort to organize black railroad porters, who had been forced to work for very low wages and tips. The brotherhood grew strong enough to win higher wages and better working conditions.

The National Negro Congress was supported by nearly all the major black organizations, and it tried to bring white and black workers together and to combat discrimination wherever it reared its head. But when Randolph and other black leaders did not follow the party line, the Communists flooded the convention of his congress with white party members who hooted Randolph down. He quit, as did most of the other black leaders, and the National Negro Congress died.

Randolph kept fighting job bias, and in 1941, with the nation on the brink of World War II, he hit upon the idea of a massive March on Washington to demand jobs in defense industries for blacks and integration of the armed forces. "Power," said Randolph, "is the active principle of only the organized masses, the masses united for a definite purpose." As his July deadline for a march on Washington approached, the black masses were organized for a show of strength, a demonstration of solidarity. Official Washington was skeptical but frightened. Mrs. Roosevelt and New York's Mayor Fiorello LaGuardia asked Randolph to call off the march, promising that some action would be taken to open up jobs for blacks. But he stood firm.

The President summoned the march's leaders to the White House and asked Walter White of the NAACP: "Walter, how many people will *really* march?"

"I told him no less than one hundred thousand," White later recalled. "The President looked me full in the eye for a long time in an obvious effort to find out if I were bluffing or exaggerating."

The last thing officials wanted were 100,000 black protesters marching on the capital. A week before the scheduled march, Roosevelt signed an executive order that forbade discrimination in defense industries and decreed government contracts must have fair employment clauses. The order set up a Fair Employment Practices Committee to investigate violations. While it had no enforcement powers and was criticized for being relatively ineffectual, the FEPC was a giant stride toward establishing the principle that equal opportunity is the federal government's business. The committee was a model for similar measures a generation later.

Roosevelt's executive order eased the situation somewhat, but the early days of the war still found black pickets marching in front of defense plants bearing placards that read:

"Bullets Know No Color Line,
Why Should Factories?"

and:

"Hitler Must Own This Plant,
Negroes Can't Work Here."

Before long, a labor-starved defense industry was opening jobs to black applicants, and by the war's end in 1945, one and one half million black workers were manning the lathes and assembly lines of the American war machine.

Fighting against Nazi racism didn't change American racism, and the home front in this second war for democracy presented some strange scenes. The NAACP's Roy Wilkins pungently commented: "It sounds pretty foolish to be *against* park benches marked 'Jude' in Berlin, but to be *for* park benches marked 'colored' in Tallahassee, Florida." Nevertheless, German prisoners of war en route to detention camps in the South were served food at restaurants and on trains, while the black soldiers guarding them either went hungry or took turns eating at Jim Crow tables. The Red Cross first refused blood from blacks and later, when its policy changed, segregated it—despite the fact that it was a black man, Dr. Charles R. Drew, who had devised the blood plasma bank and was, for a time, director of the collection of blood plasma for the armed forces.

The home front was also disrupted by riots. During the tense summer of 1943, white shipworkers rioted in Mobile, Alabama, when blacks were assigned to work alongside them in skilled jobs, and in Harlem a false rumor inflamed mobs that wrecked and looted white-owned stores. In June, Detroit broke out in the worst race riot of all. It started with fighting among whites and blacks at an amusement park, which was followed by wild rumors. As in the Chicago riot of 1919, white gangs attacked blacks in the streets and were sometimes aided by bigoted policemen, while blacks retaliated by wrecking white-owned shops in the ghetto. Within just twenty-four hours, thirty-five people lay dead, seventeen of them black victims of police bullets. It took six thousand federal troops to end the bloodshed.

As in World War I, black soldiers were victims of official discrimination. Army attitudes were reflected in official War College reports describing blacks as "careless, shiftless, irresponsible, secretive, unmoral and untruthful." As a result of this twisted thinking, blacks were once more concentrated in labor and support units. All of the services set up separate black units that were often trained in segregated facilities, often on black college campuses. The Navy limited blacks to construction battalions and the steward's branch, and the Army Air Corps was lily-white until it was pressured into creating all-black fighter squadrons. A major scandal occurred in 1943 when Judge William H. Hastie resigned his post as aide to the Secretary of War in protest against Air Corps Jim Crow policies. Unfair treatment by white officers resulted in occasional strikes and racial clashes, but despite the blatant discrimination against them, black soldiers again performed superbly in combat.

The first hero of the war was a black man, Dorie Miller. He was a messman on the battleship *Arizona,* stationed at Pearl Harbor in Hawaii on the fateful morning of December 7, 1941, when a devastating sneak attack by the Japanese brought America into the war. Miller raced on deck, manned a gun, and shot down four enemy planes. He won the Navy Cross for his valor. In 1943, he was killed in action, still a messman.

One all-black fighter group, the 332nd, flew 3,500 missions, and 88 black pilots won the Distinguished Flying Cross. The Army's black 92nd Division lost 3,000 men in combat, and its members collected 65 Silver Stars, 162 Bronze Star Medals, 1,300 Purple Hearts.

Late in the war, manpower shortages led the Army to experiment with some integrated units, and even the Navy modified its Jim Crow rules. At the war's end, black leadership was determined that blacks would never again have to serve their country in segregated units as second-class soldiers and citizens. When the peacetime draft was debated in Congress, Randolph shocked Congressmen by testifying that he would urge blacks not to serve if the law did not forbid segregation.

His campaign to end the Jim Crow Army had its effect upon the new president, Harry S. Truman, who decided to adopt a vigorous program that included anti-lynching legislation, an end to the poll tax, and a revived FEPC. Although these efforts could not pass the Congress, he issued an executive order in 1948, declaring that armed forces policy "shall be equality of treatment and opportunity for all." While the order stopped short of abolishing segregation, its meaning was clear: Jim Crow's days in uniform were numbered.

In 1951, the commander of United Nations forces in the Korean War, General Matthew B. Ridgeway, integrated black units in the combat zone. The other services soon fell into line, and by the end of that war, in 1954, nearly all black servicemen were in integrated units. Integration was accomplished swiftly and efficiently because Army discipline demanded that all officers and soldiers follow orders. Commanders could say, as one infantry colonel did: "Now men, I want you to understand this clearly because it's an order. In this integration program, there will be no trouble!"

On the civilian front, however, civil rights progress was slower. There were some breakthroughs: Jackie Robinson broke into the Brooklyn Dodgers lineup in 1947, and his success opened the doors of all professional sports to other black athletes. That same year, a special Civil Rights Committee appointed by President Truman issued a report that resulted in opening up more government jobs to blacks.

Over a period of years the Supreme Court issued a series of decisions that broadened the rights of black Americans. It outlawed the white primary in 1944 and threw out state laws requiring segregation on interstate railroads and buses in 1946. Governments were prohibited from enforcing private agreements that barred blacks from buying houses in 1948, and Jim Crow graduate and professional schools were ruled unconstitutional in 1950. Clearly, the Court was moving, in its traditionally slow and hesitant manner, to a re-examination of the "separate but equal" doctrine that had reigned unchallenged since 1896.

Jim Crow was most vulnerable to attack in the separate school systems of the South. No matter how much the state and federal courts would have liked to hold the "separate but equal" line, inequality was glaringly apparent. Mississippi in 1949 was spending a mere $26.81 per pupil in its black schools, compared with $122.74 per white pupil. Other Deep South states were also spending two and three times as much on white schools as on black ones.

A black man in Topeka, Kansas, Oliver Brown, tried to enroll his daughter in an all-white school just five blocks from his home. He was rebuffed, and his child was forced to travel twenty-one blocks to attend an all-black school. Brown sued, but the court ruled that Topeka's Jim Crow schools were legal. NAACP lawyers, headed by Thurgood Marshall, took the case to the Supreme Court, where it joined similar challenges to segregated schools.

On May 17, 1954, the nine black-robed justices filed into a packed courtroom to give their verdict. Chief Justice Earl Warren delivered the unanimous opinion. "Segregation of white and colored children in public schools has a detrimental effect upon the colored children," Warren said, for it "generates a feeling of inferiority as to their status in the community that may affect their hearts and minds in a way unlikely ever to be undone. . . . We conclude," said the Chief Justice of the United States, "that in the field of public education the doctrine of 'separate but equal' has no place. Separate educational facilities are inherently unequal."

Although Marshall, who was later to sit on the Court himself, argued that it should order complete desegregation of the South's separate school systems no later than the September 1956 term, the Court, in 1955, decided that school integration should only proceed "with all deliberate speed." The following years brought more deliberateness than speed, but the Court had taken a decisive step, one that was to usher in a period of social ferment and basic reform unseen in American race relations since the days of Reconstruction.

15. The Second Reconstruction

Rosa Parks was tired. Late one December afternoon in 1955, she boarded the Cleveland Avenue bus after a long day's work in a leading Montgomery, Alabama, department store. She walked past the "white" section and took a seat in the Jim Crow rear of the bus. A few stops later, some white passengers got on, saw that all the seats were taken, and looked at the driver. "Let me have those seats," the driver ordered, and three black people got up and made way for the whites.

Rosa Parks stayed put. "My shoulder ached, I had a bad day at work," she recalled, "I was tired from sewing all day, and all of a sudden, everything was just too much. It didn't seem logical, particularly for a woman to give way to a man. I had paid the same fare. I stayed where I was." The police were called, and Rosa Parks was taken to the city jail, where she was booked for violating Montgomery's Jim Crow laws.

There was nothing unusual about this incident. Other black people all over the South had been arrested in similar circumstances. But this time something different happened. The phones buzzed as black leaders angrily discussed what might be done. "Another black woman has been arrested for refusing to give up her seat on a bus. We've got to do something." It was decided to stage a bus boycott. Handbills flooded the black community: "Don't ride the bus to work, to town, to school, or anyplace Monday, December 5." The buses were empty that day. Blacks walked, rode mules, hitchhiked rides in private cars, but none rode the buses.

In the evening there was a mass meeting at the Holt Street Baptist Church. A full two hours before it started every seat was taken, and blacks lined the walls and jammed the aisles. More than three thousand people milled about in front of the church, listening to loudspeakers that had been set up. A young black minister, the Reverend Dr. Martin Luther King, Jr., stood to address the throng.

"There comes a time," he said, "when people get tired. We are here this evening to say to those who have mistreated us so long that we are tired—tired of being segregated and humiliated; tired of being kicked about by the brutal feet of oppression. We had no alternative but to protest. For many years we have shown amazing patience. . . . But we come here tonight to be saved from that patience that makes us patient with anything less than freedom and justice."

Montgomery's black people had found a leader. For more than a year, guided by a committee of ministers and community leaders headed by Dr. King, they shunned the buses. They walked; they took taxis; they shared in a special three hundred car pool. But they did not take the buses.

An angry city government arrested Martin Luther King, unifying Montgomery's blacks all the more. Then, in

January, when King was at another mass meeing, a bomb tore away the front of his house. His wife and child escaped injury, and thousands of furious armed blacks gathered in front of the house. The city seemed on the verge of violence and bloodshed.

King arrived, and, with television cameras whirring, he pleaded with the crowd. "Don't get panicky. Don't get your weapons. He who lives by the sword will perish by the sword. We are not advocating violence. I want you to love our enemies. Be good to them. Love them and let them know you love them." The tension broke, the crowd went home. Dr. King's message of love and nonviolent action spread across the country, and Montgomery's black leader became the man who gripped the imagination of the nation, destined to be the voice of black people in their struggle for justice.

In 1956, when the Supreme Court ruled bus segregation unconstitutional and the boycott ended in triumph, King was just twenty-seven years old. What kind of man was this prophet of nonviolence who beseeched a crowd to love its enemies while standing amidst the wreckage of his bombed-out home? He grew up in a comfort known by few blacks in the South. His father was the minister of an important Atlanta church, and young Martin studied philosophy and theology, earning a doctorate from Boston University.

He had long been attracted to pacifism and was deeply impressed by the nonviolent philosophy of Ghandi, who organized the masses of India to overthrow British rule by moral force, without resort to arms. "Nonviolent resistance is not a method for cowards," Martin Luther King argued. "It does resist." It attacks the evil, not the "persons who happen to be doing the evil," he held. King was concerned that violent resistance would result in "internal violence of the spirit"; by fighting fire with fire, one lowers himself morally to the same level as the oppressor.

Many people, even those sympathetic to the black man's cause, questioned any resistance to laws, violent or nonviolent. Black people, they said, should fight injustice in the courts and in the Congress, not in the streets. But King, in an open letter from a jail cell in Birmingham, Alabama, in 1963, explained his tactic of mass demonstrations against evil laws. Citing Saint Augustine, he wrote, "An unjust law is no law at all." Such a law, Martin Luther King declared, "is a code inflicted upon a minority which that minority had no part in enacting or creating."

"Nonviolent direct action seeks to create such a crisis and establish such creative tension that a community that has consistently refused to negotiate is forced to confront the issue. It seeks so to dramatize the issue that it can no longer be ingored." Society, he explained, needs the kind of tension "that will help men to rise from the dark depths of prejudice and racism to the heights of understanding and brotherhood."

He based his appeal for justice on Christian morality and the suffering and struggle that enobles the oppressed. Like Douglass and Du Bois, he demanded complete equality for blacks. "We know through painful experience," King wrote, "that freedom is never voluntarily given by the oppressor; it must be demanded by the oppressed." The South that King faced had no intention of granting equality voluntarily. It dug in its heels and resisted black demands and federal laws.

The Supreme Court's decision banning segregated

schools was openly ignored. Governors swore they would never integrate schools. The Klan and the White Citizens' Councils spread, and soon bombs ripped the homes of black leaders and destroyed integrated school buildings. Alabama banned the NAACP, and blacks trying to organize civil rights activities faced a stepped-up campaign of harassment. Riots occurred when black students, armed with court orders, tried to attend universities in Georgia and Alabama. Mobs of screaming, club-waving whites gathered to frighten black children on their way to integrated schools.

In 1957, when Little Rock's Central High School was opened to black students, Arkansas Governor Orval Faubus called out the National Guard "to maintain order." The real purpose was to prevent integration. Fifteen-year-old Elizabeth Eckford walked through the mob in front of Central High and approached the guard at the entrance. "He raised his bayonet and then the other guards closed in and they raised their bayonets," she remembered. "They glared at me with a mean look and I was very frightened." Elizabeth escaped unharmed, the cries of a mob yelling, "Lynch her! Lynch her!" ringing in her ears.

President Dwight D. Eisenhower, who had never publicly approved of the Supreme Court's integration decision, saying that "laws can't change the hearts of men," could not ignore this flagrant violation of federal court orders. He sent a thousand paratroops into Little Rock and forced the integration of the school.

In 1960, the civil rights revolution moved into a new phase. Four well-dressed black college students walked into a five-and-dime store in Greensboro, North Carolina, and sat down at a lunch counter. "We buy books and papers in the other part of the store. We should get served in this part," said their spokesman. Black and white shoppers looked on in amazement. That blacks and whites could not eat together at the same table was close to the heart of Jim Crow. The manager closed the counter rather than serve them.

The next day they came back; and the day after; and the day after that. Television viewers throughout the nation saw them sitting patiently, waiting for service that never came. The lunacy of Jim Crow law and custom was brought into the living rooms of millions of Americans, who watched the sit-ins with admiration for the brave young people who demanded their rights. The movement spread like wildfire. Within two weeks the sit-ins had spread to fifteen other cities. Within a year, some fifty thousand whites and blacks had taken part in a sit-in or a similar protest.

White mobs often attacked the demonstrators. White students who took part in integrated protests were special targets. Hot coffee was spilled on them; cigarette butts were ground out on their necks. Some were pulled off stools and beaten. But they were nonviolent. They didn't fight back. They were true to King's philosophy, and their courage won support from white people all over the country. Thousands of young people were jailed, but they wore their imprisonment proudly, as a badge of honor. "Try to understand that what I am doing is right," wrote one boy to his parents. "It isn't like going to jail for a crime like stealing or killing, but we are going for the betterment of all Negroes."

In 1961, another attack was mounted, this time on

segregation in interstate bus travel. Led by James Farmer, head of CORE (Congress of Racial Equality), an integrated group set out on a bus ride through the South to demonstrate the existence of illegal segregation. Angry crowds armed with clubs and bottles met them where they stopped. They were brutally beaten. One of their buses was burned. But still they went on, winding their way through a South filled with hatred. At one point, six hundred federal marshalls had to be mobilized to protect them. They made their point. The government moved quickly to end segregation in buses and terminals.

Federal troops also had to be called out in 1962, to enforce a court order instructing the University of Mississippi to admit James Meredith as a student. Egged on by Governor Ross Barnett and other politicians who courted racist votes, howling whites rioted, attacking federal marshalls and newsmen.

These events created a sense of moral outrage in the nation. Black demands were elementary—the right to eat at a public lunch counter, the right to ride in a bus, the right to attend a school. When these demands were presented with dignity and nonviolent determination and were met by increased oppression and violence, sympathy and support for black people spread. Martin Luther King's strategy of militant nonviolence was working.

The nation, however, was in for more shocks, more brutality. In the spring of 1963, Dr. King led mass demonstrations in Birmingham, in a campaign for jobs and an end to segregation in downtown stores. King was arrested early in the campaign, and the policemen under chief Eugene "Bull" Connor waded into kneeling, praying demonstrators, billy clubs flying.

With two thousand demonstrators and their leaders in jail, it looked as though the battle of Birmingham would end in defeat, but then it was the children's turn. For nearly a week, black children marched singing and shouting toward police barricades barring their way. Connor's policemen used their clubs, dogs, and high-pressure fire hoses to beat them back. When the world's newspapers featured pictures of razor-toothed police dogs attacking black children, the twisted face of racist repression became clear to all. As President John F. Kennedy was later to say: "The civil rights movement owes 'Bull' Connor as much as it owes Abraham Lincoln."

Martin Luther King tightened the screws, the pressures mounted, and finally Birmingham gave in. An agreement was reached, but within days four black children lay dead, the victims of a bomb blast that destroyed a black church. Such wholesale violence was becoming an increasing part of the southern way of life. Churches and synagogues were bombed and civil rights workers murdered.

Medgar Evers, the head of the NAACP in Mississippi, was murdered. His killer was not convicted. During the selection of the jury at his trial, an attorney asked a prospective juror, "Do you think it's a crime for a white man to kill a nigger in Mississippi?"

"What was his answer?" asked the judge.

"He's thinking it over," answered the lawyer.

In 1964, three young rights workers were killed during the Freedom Summer campaign—a drive by white and black students from all over the country to organize Mississippi blacks to register and vote. After a mass search by federal agents, the bodies of the three—Andrew Goodman, Michael Schwerner, and James Chaney—were found buried beneath a mound of red clay. Twenty-one white men were arrested for the murders, including the sheriff and deputy sheriff of Neshoba County and several Klan leaders. Besides the three murders, the four-month long Freedom Summer claimed other casualties. Eighty rights workers were beaten, three wounded in thirty-five shooting incidents, thirty-five churches burned, thirty buildings bombed, and more than a thousand arrested.

Racism exacted a bitter price for the effort to win civil rights for all. But the effort to combat it resulted in a movement that brought whites and blacks together as never before in our history. Most whites sat on the sidelines, observers of the tragedy of their nation's history. But the few who fought tooth and nail to preserve white supremacy were balanced by the many who linked arms with their black brothers and marched for freedom. The fervor and righteousness of the cause awoke countless white people, especially the young, to reaffirm the ideals of brotherhood and justice.

This movement came to full flower in the summer of 1963, when 250,000 people—white and black—left their homes and jobs to march on Washington to demand federal action for jobs and equal rights. The march was organized by the major civil rights organizations and was headed by the aging A. Philip Randolph, whose idea it was. Randolph's aide, Bayard Rustin, was in charge of the massive task of ensuring an orderly and peaceful demonstration.

The crowd, the largest ever seen in Washington, stretched for almost a mile in front of the Lincoln Memorial, where speaker after speaker called for "Freedom, NOW." But the day was Martin Luther King's. In his Baptist preacher's cadence, he hypnotized the masses at his feet and the millions watching on television. "I have a dream," he declared. "I have a dream that one day this nation will rise up and live out the true meaning of its creed. . . . I have a dream that one day on the red hills of Georgia the sons of former slaves and the sons of former slaveowners will be able to sit down together at the table of brotherhood. . . .

"I have a dream that one day even the state of Mississippi, a state sweltering with the people's injustice, sweltering with the heat of oppression, will be transformed into an oasis of freedom and justice. . . . I have a dream that my four little children will one day live in a nation where they will not be judged by the color of their skin, but by the content of their character. . . .

"This is our hope. This is the faith with which I return to the South. . . . With this faith we will be able to hew out of the mountain of despair a stone of hope."

When he finished, the huge crowd, people of all colors and beliefs, linked arms and sang the anthem of the civil rights movement:

> "We shall overcome
> We shall overcome
> We shall overcome someday.
> Deep in my heart I do believe
> We shall overcome someday."

Their voices rang out, rising above the Lincoln Memorial, seeping into the halls of Congress, the White House, and the nation—and they were heard. In 1964, the Congress passed the strongest civil rights legislation since Reconstruction days. It barred discrimination in most public places such as restaurants and hotels, increased the government's power to fight discrimination in schools and other public facilities, and required an end to discrimination in federally assisted programs.

The next step was to win the ballot for blacks in the South. Despite some Supreme Court decisions and a 1957 Civil Rights Act aimed at eliminating some of the more flagrant abuses of voting rights, many parts of the Deep South still kept blacks from voting. Sometimes the method used was intimidation—firing blacks who tried to register or refusing them store credit. Sometimes the methods were more subtle. Black college professors were failed in literacy tests, and black voters were disqualified for something like circling a box on the registration form instead of checking it.

The spark that led to federal action was a demonstration led by Dr. King in Selma, Alabama, to protest the arrest of one thousand people in a voter registration campaign. State troopers armed with tear gas, clubs, and whips turned King's demonstrators back. Some were beaten, a white minister was killed. King's response was to call for a march from Selma to the state capital in Montgomery.

When Governor George Wallace refused to defend the forty thousand marchers from violence, President Lyndon B. Johnson mobilized the state's National Guard. The march was a success, as troops lined the route and Army helicopters followed in the air. Then tragedy struck once more. Klansmen pumped bullets into a car returning from the Montgomery rally and killed its driver, Mrs. Viola Gregg Liuzzo, a white mother of five, from Detroit.

The national revulsion resulted in passage of another

key piece of legislation of the second Reconstruction—
the Voting Rights Act of 1965. The act suspended literacy tests and other rules used to discriminate against blacks
in southern counties where fewer than half of the adults
had voted in 1964. Where local authorities were not register-
ing people according to the law, the Attorney General was
authorized to send federal registrars to do the job. Federal
agents were immediately dispatched to several hard-core
segregationist counties, and long lines of black men and
women jammed their offices to take the ballot so long
denied to them.

The Voting Rights Act and massive voter registration
drives by civil rights organizations changed the political
face of the South. Mississippi, which had a mere 22,000
blacks registered to vote in 1960, had 300,000 registered
blacks in 1970. In the course of the decade, states such as
Alabama and South Carolina quadrupled their black voters. Furthermore, black political power became a moderat-
ing influence on many white politicians, who recognized
that the old, all-out appeals to racism might bring defeat at
the polls.

Throughout the Black Belt, blacks were now holding
office. They were sheriffs, town councillors, county officers,
and even mayors. Charles Evers, brother of the slain Medgar Evers, was elected mayor of Fayette, Mississippi, in
1969.

Blacks also held important federal posts. Robert
Weaver became the first black member of the Cabinet, when
he was appointed Secretary of Housing and Urban Development in 1966. And in the following year, President
Johnson named Thurgood Marshall, the hero of innumera-

ble NAACP civil rights suits, as the first black justice of the Supreme Court. Such appointments were symbolic of the national concern for equal rights. "Their cause must be our cause too," President Johnson told Congress. "It is not just Negroes, but all of us, who must overcome the crippling legacy of bigotry and injustice." Then, echoing the anthem of the rights movement, he said: "And we *shall* overcome."

Presidents Kennedy and Johnson placed federal power squarely behind equal rights, but somehow, it just was not enough. What did it matter if the law now said a man could eat at a lunch counter or stay at a fancy hotel if he did not have the price of a sandwich or of a room? And what was the right to vote when, after casting his ballot, a man returned to a rundown shack to look at his malnourished children? The newly won rights were important, but their full potential for changing the system that excluded black people was still to be fulfilled.

The rhetoric of equality was not followed by the kinds of results that would give it substance. And attacks on southern segregation meant little to the black millions who suffered discrimination in northern ghettos. The concern and activity of the rights movement had intensified black awareness of white injustice, while also bringing rising expectations that conditions would change radically—and soon. When that did not happen, frustration turned to anger, and bitterness to violence.

In the summer of 1965, shortly after the passage of the Voting Rights Act, the predominately black Watts area of Los Angeles erupted in a riot triggered by rough police handling of a crowd during an arrest. For five days, stores were looted and buildings burned. When thirteen thousand

National Guardsmen finally restored order, thirty-four were dead, a thousand injured, and property damage was estimated at $40 million.

The Watts riot was similar to others in the "long, hot summers" of the mid-1960s. The first of these was the Harlem riot of 1964, which started when an off-duty policeman killed a black teen-ager, and many of those that followed were caused by some incident of real or imagined police brutality or insensitivity. Once riots started, badly trained police forces often made them worse through indiscriminate shooting, reports of imaginary sniper attacks, and occasional instances of retaliatory shootings and clubbings.

Some of the worst riots took place in 1967. Newark, where proportionately three times as many blacks as whites were unemployed, leading to ghetto poverty and anger, boiled over in July. The toll: twenty-six dead, a thousand injured. No sooner had the flames of Newark cooled than Detroit broke loose. Regular Army troops were flown in, but by then forty-three people were dead and over two thousand injured.

Few cities escaped the torch in those turbulent summers. Violence and counter-violence replaced reason and progress, and the nation wondered where it had gone astray. In 1967, a National Advisory Commission on Civil Disorders was appointed to investigate the riots and make recommendations to prevent them in the future.

"This is our basic conclusion," the commission's report stated. "Our nation is moving toward two societies, one black, one white—separate and unequal." It laid the blame for the riots on the segregation and poverty that "created in the ghetto a destructive environment unknown to most white Americans." "White society," the report continued, "is deeply implicated in the ghetto. White institutions created it, white institutions maintain it, and white society condones it." Later presidential commissions appointed to investigate violence, crime, automation, and other social problems reached similar conclusions. All agreed that massive action to create jobs and to provide better housing and education were essential.

Black leaders had been calling for such measures for a long time. In 1963, the National Urban League's dynamic leader, Whitney M. Young, Jr., proposed a domestic Marshall Plan that would bring economic equality to black people. It was to be modeled on the original Marshall Plan, the American aid program that restored Western Europe after World War II. Federal efforts to eliminate poverty, however, fell far short of Marshall plan proportions. The Johnson Administration launched a "War on Poverty" that was actually more of a skirmish, committing far smaller funds than were needed to make a dent in the problem.

Job-training programs and similar efforts brought few tangible results. And the war in Vietnam, the first in United States history in which black soldiers were completely integrated in all services and at all levels of command, drained the economy so badly that federal housing and education programs were drastically cut back. Dr. King, himself a Nobel Peace Prize winner, led the growing opposition to the war, pointing out its damaging moral and economic effects.

The recommendations of the National Advisory Commission on Civil Disorders went largely unheeded. The black educator Dr. Kenneth B. Clark foresaw the results in his testimony before the commission: "I read that report . . . of the 1919 riot in Chicago, and it is as if I were reading the report of the investigating committee on the Harlem riot of '35, the report of the investigating committee on the Harlem riot of '43, the report of the McCone Commission on the Watts riot. . . . It is a kind of Alice in Wonderland—with the same moving picture shown over and over again, the same analysis, the same recommendations, and the same inaction." As in the first Reconstruction a century earlier, activity and progress ground to a halt after a few short years.

When the civil rights movement turned its attention to the North, where informal segregation was almost as rigid as the state-supported southern variety, many sympathetic whites backed off. They were willing to open public places to blacks or to support blacks in their quest for the right to vote, but when it came to having blacks moving next door or going to *their* children's schools or joining *their* unions or demanding equal jobs in *their* factories or offices, resistance became stiff. As in the 1870s, northern whites abandoned the cause of black equality, and many came to see black people as a threat to their security and status. This white backlash was given impetus by the riots and by the growing mood of anger and militancy among blacks.

The model for many young militants became not Martin Luther King, Jr., with his nonviolence and brotherly love, but the black nationalist Malcolm X, who once scornfully derided King, telling blacks: "You need somebody who is going to fight. You don't need any kneeling-in or crawling-in."

Malcolm was born Malcolm Little. When he was still a

child, his father, a follower of Marcus Garvey, was murdered by the Black Legion, a white racist group modeled after the Klan. Malcolm grew up a drifter, a petty hoodlum, and a criminal. In prison, where he was serving a sentence for burglary, he became a convert to the Black Muslims, a sect that combined what it thought to be Islam with its own ideas about the origin of the world and of the races, and with a separatist black nationalism.

Malcolm quickly rose to a position of leadership in the organization. His articulate presentations of Black Muslim ideology and his attacks on whites as "blue-eyed devils" won him national attention. His anger, his humor, his ability to punch holes in the irrational racism of the society won him a large following among blacks who did not accept his religion. He later split with the Muslims, traveled to Mecca and to Africa, and returned with his militant nationalism intact, but softened by a less rigid attitude toward white people.

In 1965, Malcolm was shot down at a public meeting. No one can tell how he would have developed his changing ideology, or what role he might have played as a militant black leader. But his influence among the young is great. His definition of America as a "prison" won believers, and his outspoken advocacy of violent self-defense became a cardinal creed of groups such as the Black Panthers and other extreme militants that sprung up in the late sixties. If a white man "only understands the language of a rifle, get a rifle," he said. "If he only understands the language of a rope, get a rope. But don't waste time talking the wrong language to a man if you really want to communicate with him."

Such statements fueled the flames of anger in the hearts of black people who were outraged at the oppression they suffered. But there is another side to Malcolm, one which he revealed in his last months, when he abandoned his call for a separate black nation and even stopped using the term "black nationalism." Where he had once scorned political action, he now declared: "Don't be throwing out any ballots. A ballot is like a bullet. . . . I believe in political action." And he described the Organization of Afro-American Unity, the group he founded in 1964 after his break with the Muslims, as "an all-black organization whose ultimate objective was to help create a society in which there could exist honest white-black brotherhood." Malcolm's untimely death removed from the scene an outstanding militant spokesman who might have continued to grow and who might have been able to bridge the gap between the nationalist sector of black opinion and those still committed to working within the framework of present-day society.

Malcolm's speeches and his *Autobiography* were read avidly, as were other black writings—both fiction and non-fiction. Eldridge Cleaver's prison essays *Soul on Ice,* like Malcolm's writings, attacked racism and preached black pride and unity in the struggle against a society that oppressed blacks. James Baldwin's novels and essays combined anger with a poetic touch missing in most other writing of the period—black or white—making him the most popular black author since Richard Wright, whose 1940 novel *Native Son* was a powerful drama of black anger in Depression Chicago. The writings of Ralph Ellison and the plays of Lorraine Hansberry made a deep impact on white audiences. At the same time, the turmoil of the civil rights struggle led to a resurgence of black writing in the sixties that dealt with ghetto bitterness and racial strife. John Williams, LeRoi Jones, and a host of young novelists, playwrights, and poets spearheaded the new literary movement, and urban ghettos sprouted writer's workshops and drama groups, producing works of fierce pride and no little talent.

Black musicians continued to dominate popular culture, although their white imitators were often better known and made more money. This was an old story. The great jazz bands of the thirties—Duke Ellington, Count Basie, and others—never became as popular with the public as white orchestras whom they influenced. The success of Benny Goodman's jazz orchestra in that period owed much to arrangements by Fletcher Henderson, whose own all-black band had failed financially. So, too, in the sixties, the hard-driving rhythms and searing lyrics of black blues singers served as the basis for rock music, which was brought to the white public by American and English groups. Yet black bluesmen such as Ray Charles, black "soul" singers like Aretha Franklin and James Brown, and black jazzmen like John Coltrane still reached large audiences while maintaining the pure, burning heat of ghetto-based music. Their work reflected the long traditions of emotion and intensity of performance, and their art, like that of black poets and novelists, formed the cultural edge of the black thrust for power and recognition.

"Black Power" became the phrase that embodied the aspirations of the militants and the fears of many whites. The concept came into national prominence in 1966. James Meredith, whose attempts to enter the University of Mississippi four years earlier had touched off a white riot, started a lone march through the back roads of Mississippi. He called it a march against fear, a demonstration of courage that would spur Mississippi blacks to conquer their fears of white reprisals and vote. He had walked only ten miles into the state when shots rang out and he fell sprawling. The wounded Meredith was taken to a Memphis hospital, but civil rights leaders from across the country assembled to continue his march. With television cameras and newspaper reporters on the scene, the tense caravan, led by Dr. King, made its way through the state. Stokely Carmichael, the young leader of SNCC (Student Nonviolent Coordinating Committee) started shouting "Black Power," and crowds at meetings along the line of march picked it up.

In that tense atmosphere of racial conflict, the phrase was loaded with emotional meaning, open to hopeful interpretations by blacks and terrifying ones by whites. As time passed, the phrase lost much of its emotionalism. All blacks came to embrace it as meaning that they should have a full share of the economic and political power in America—something none could contest.

SNCC, CORE, and other black-power organizations, however, interpreted black power quite differently. They expelled white members and called for an all-black movement. The long-smoldering tensions between white liberals and blacks had surfaced. Many black civil rights workers were resentful of the bright young white students who came to help, but flaunted their Ivy League backgrounds and dominated rural voter drives or organization campaigns. The split recalled the tensions between white and black abolitionists in the nineteenth century.

Although organizations such as the NAACP and the

235

Urban League remained firmly committed to interracial co-operation, they, too, were affected by the new militancy and the trend toward unifying the black ghetto. In 1968, the Urban League announced a "New Thrust"—changing its primary task from job-finding and dealing with business to one of intensive organization in the ghetto. Many whites also remained firm in their commitment to black equality, but others, disillusioned by "black power" and conscious of other ills in American society, abandoned the civil rights cause to campaign against the Vietnam War or against environmental pollution.

The second Reconstruction was almost spent—its last gasp may have been a law passed in 1968 outlawing housing discrimination. But the law was passed in a mood of national shame over the loss of the primary symbol of the period's progress—Dr. Martin Luther King, Jr.

Early in 1968, Dr. King went to Memphis to support black sanitation men in their strike for union recognition and an end to discrimination. On the evening of April 4, he stepped out onto the balcony of his motel room. Leaning over a railing, he joked casually with some friends below. A shot rang out. He toppled over. Within minutes he was dead. Adviser to presidents, Nobel Prize winner, leader of the black masses, idol of the idealistic pursuers of justice of both races, the apostle of nonviolence and love was dead.

Did justice die with him? A shocked nation, shamed by his death, shamed by the violence that claimed President Kennedy in 1963 and his brother Robert F. Kennedy in 1968, shamed by a war no one wanted and a race problem no one knew how to resolve, asked the question—and waited for an answer.

The story of black Americans is crowded with martyrs like Dr. King. It is a story of unending struggle, of periods of cooperation with whites for the common good, followed by periods of white withdrawals and oppression. It is a story of hope and a story of disillusionment, anger, and bitterness.

Black people helped build America. Stolen from the African homeland, they came in chains to till the soil, fell the trees, construct the roads of a new nation. Their blood, sweat, and tears helped turn a virgin land into an industrial power. Black inventors, artisans, explorers, artists, statesmen, and entrepreneurs gave America important and vital contributions in all fields. Black artists, musicians, and common people gave America something else distinctively their own, something called soul.

In the early 1970s, the withdrawal of blacks and whites from common efforts to create an open society is reminiscent of other periods of withdrawal and separatism. But these periods ended, and the wheel of history turned full circle, once again bringing progress and temporary unity. This change, though, is not inevitable. The forces opposed to black equality are entrenched, and history's wheel turns only when men—determined and committed—push it. At times, the struggle seems like that of Sysiphus, hero of an ancient myth, who was doomed to pushing a heavy rock to the top of a mountain, only to watch it roll down again, and whose fate it was to repeat the process endlessly.

Dr. King's death, the riots that followed it, and the deepening social tensions and economic problems were met with no action to change the system that keeps black citizens relatively powerless and poor in a society both powerful and rich. As the nation entered the seventies, it seemed totally indifferent to the plight of its poor and its minorities. Black economic gains remained limited, and repression grew. Hopefully the wheel will again turn, and blacks and whites will again work together, trying to raise from the ashes of the past a society dedicated to the equality of all men, a society that encourages diversity and brings an end to mistrust and fear and racism.

Selected Bibliography

Aptheker, Herbert. *American Negro Slave Revolts*. New York: International Publications, 1963.

Aptheker, Herbert, ed. *A Documentary History of the Negro People in the United States*. New York: Citadel, 1966.

Balandier, Georges. *Daily Life in the Kingdom of the Kongo*. New York: Pantheon, 1968.

Blaustein, Albert P., and Zangrando, Robert L., eds. *Civil Rights and the Black American*. New York: Clarion, 1968.

Bontemps, Arna, ed. *American Negro Poetry*. New York: Hill & Wang, 1963.

Bontemps, Arna, ed. *Great Slave Narratives*. Boston: Beacon, 1969.

Breitman, George, ed. *Malcolm X Speaks*. New York: Grove, 1966.

Broderick, Francis L., and Meier, August, eds. *Negro Protest Thought in the Twentieth Century*. Indianapolis: Bobbs-Merrill, 1965.

Chalmers, David M. *Hooded Americanism*. Garden City, N.Y.: Doubleday, 1965.

Cronon, Edmund David. *Black Moses: The Story of Marcus Garvey and the Universal Negro Improvement Association*. Madison: University of Wisconsin Press, 1966.

239

Selected Bibliography

Dalfiume, Richard M. *Desegregation of the United States Armed Forces.* Columbia, Mo.: University of Missouri Press, 1969.

Davidson, Basil, ed. *The African Past: Chronicles from Antiquity to Modern Times.* New York: Grosset Universal Library, 1967.

Davidson, Basil. *Black Mother: The Years of the African Slave Trade.* Boston: Little Brown, 1961.

Davidson, Basil. *A History of West Africa to the Nineteenth Century.* Garden City, N.Y.: Anchor, 1969.

Donnan, Elizabeth, ed. *Documents Illustrative of the History of the Slave Trade to America.* New York: Octagon, 1965.

Douglass, Frederick. *Life and Times of Frederick Douglass.* New York: Collier, 1962.

Draper, Theodore. *The Rediscovery of Black Nationalism.* New York: Viking, 1970.

Drimmer, Melvin, ed. *Black History: A Reappraisal.* Garden City, N.Y.: Doubleday, 1968.

Du Bois, W. E. B. *Black Reconstruction in America, 1860–1880.* New York: Atheneum, 1969.

Durham, Philip, and Jones, Everett L. *The Negro Cowboys.* New York: Dodd, Mead, 1965.

Eaton, Clement. *A History of the Southern Confederacy.* New York: Collier, 1962.

Elkins, Stanley. *Slavery: A Problem in American Institutional and Intellectual Life.* Chicago: University of Chicago Press, 1959.

Filler, Louis. *The Crusade Against Slavery, 1830–1860.* New York: Harper Torchbook, 1960.

Fishel, Leslie H., Jr., and Quarles, Benjamin, eds. *The Black American: A Documentary History.* New York: Morrow, 1970.

Foner, Philip S. *Frederick Douglass.* New York: Citadel, 1964.

Franklin, John Hope. *The Emancipation Proclamation.* Garden City, N.Y.: Anchor, 1965.

Franklin, John Hope. *From Slavery to Freedom.* New York: Knopf, 1967.

Garfinkel, Herbert. *When Negroes March.* New York: Atheneum, 1969.

Garvey, Amy Jacques, ed. *Philosophy and Opinions of Marcus Garvey.* New York: Humanities Press, 1968.

Genovese, Eugene D. *The Political Economy of Slavery.* New York: Pantheon, 1965.

Grant, Joanne, ed. *Black Protest: History, Documents and Analyses from Sixteen Nineteen to the Present.* New York: Fawcett, 1968.

Greene, Lorenzo Johnston. *The Negro in Colonial New England.* New York: Atheneum, 1968.

Herskovits, Melville J. *The Myth of the Negro Past.* Boston: Beacon, 1958.

Hoover, Dwight W., ed. *Understanding Negro History.* Chicago: Quadrangle, 1968.

Jacobson, Julius, ed. *The Negro and the American Labor Movement.* Garden City, N.Y.: Anchor, 1968.

Jordan, Winthrop D. *White Over Black: American Attitudes Toward the Negro, 1550–1812.* Chapel Hill: University of North Carolina Press, 1968.

Kirwan, Albert D. *The Revolt of the Rednecks: Mississippi Politics, 1876–1925.* New York: Harper Torchbook, 1965.

Lewinson, Paul. *Race, Class & Party.* New York: Grosset Universal Library, 1965.

Lewis, Anthony, and New York Times Editors. *Portrait of a Decade.* New York: Bantam, 1965.

Lewis, David L. *King: A Critical Biography.* New York: Praeger, 1970.

Selected Bibliography

Litwack, Leon F. *North of Slavery: The Negro in the Free States, 1790–1860.* Chicago: University of Chicago Press, 1961.

Locke, Alain, ed. *The New Negro.* New York: Atheneum, 1968.

Logan, Rayford W. *The Betrayal of the Negro, from Rutherford B. Hayes to Woodrow Wilson.* New York: Collier, 1965.

Malcolm X. *The Autobiography of Malcolm X.* New York: Grove, 1965.

Mannix, Daniel P., and Cowley, Malcolm. *Black Cargoes: A History of the Atlantic Slave Trade.* New York: Viking, 1962.

McKitrick, Eric L. *Andrew Johnson and Reconstruction.* Chicago: University of Chicago Press, 1960.

McPherson, James M., ed. *The Negro's Civil War.* New York: Vintage, 1965.

McPherson, James M. *The Struggle for Equality: Abolitionists and the Negro in the Civil War and Reconstruction.* Princeton: Princeton University Press, 1964.

Meier, August, and Rudwick, Elliott M., eds. *The Making of Black America.* New York: Atheneum, 1969.

Meier, August. *Negro Thought in America, 1880–1915.* Ann Arbor: University of Michigan Press, 1963.

Myrdal, Gunnar. *An American Dilemma: The Negro Problem and Modern Democracy.* New York: Harper, 1962.

National Advisory Commission on Civil Disorders. *Report of the National Advisory Commission on Civil Disorders.* New York: Dutton, 1968.

Nichols, Charles H. *Many Thousand Gone: The Ex-Slaves' Account of Their Bondage and Freedom.* Bloomington: University of Indiana Press, 1969.

Oliver, Roland, and Oliver, Caroline. *Africa in the Days of Exploration.* Englewood Cliffs, N.J.: Prentice-Hall, 1965.

Selected Bibliography

Osofsky, Gilbert, ed. *The Burden of Race: A Documentary History of Negro-White Relations in America*. New York: Harper & Row, 1967.

Osofsky, Gilbert. *Harlem: The Making of a Ghetto*. New York: Harper & Row, 1966.

Ottley, Roi, and Weatherby, William J., eds. *The Negro in New York: An Informal Social History, 1626–1940*. New York: Praeger, 1969.

Quarles, Benjamin. *Black Abolitionists*. New York: Oxford, 1969.

Quarles, Benjamin. *The Negro in the American Revolution*. Chapel Hill: University of North Carolina Press, 1961.

Redkey, Edwin S. *Black Exodus: Black Nationalist and Back-to-Africa Movements, 1890–1910*. New Haven: Yale University Press, 1969.

Spear, Allan H. *Black Chicago: The Making of a Negro Ghetto, 1890–1920*. Chicago: University of Chicago Press, 1967.

Stampp, Kenneth M. *The Era of Reconstruction: 1865–1877*. New York: Vintage, 1967.

Stampp, Kenneth M. *The Peculiar Institution*. New York: Vintage, 1964.

Stampp, Kenneth M., and Litwack, Leon F., eds. *Reconstruction: An Anthology of Revisionist Writings*. Baton Rouge: Louisiana State University Press, 1969.

Sternsher, Bernard, ed. *The Negro in Depression and War: Prelude to Revolution*. Chicago: Quadrangle, 1969.

Stillman, Richard J. *Integration of the Negro in the U.S. Armed Forces*. New York: Praeger, 1968.

Tannenbaum, Frank. *Slave and Citizen: The Negro in the Americas*. New York: Vintage, 1963.

Trefousse, Hans L. *The Radical Republicans: Lincoln's Vanguard for Racial Justice*. New York: Knopf, 1969.

Selected Bibliography

Wade, Richard C. *Slavery in the Cities: The South 1820–1860.* New York: Oxford, 1967.

Waskow, Arthur I. *From Race Riot to Sit-In, 1919 and the 1960s.* Garden City, N.Y.: Anchor, 1967.

Watters, Pat, and Cleghorn, Reese. *Climbing Jacob's Ladder: The Arrival of Negroes in Southern Politics.* New York: Harcourt Brace Jovanovich, 1967.

Weinberg, Meyer, ed. *W. E. B. Du Bois, a Reader.* New York: Harper Torchbook, 1970.

Weinstein, Allen, and Gatell, Frank Otto, eds. *American Negro Slavery: A Modern Reader.* New York: Oxford, 1968.

Weinstein, Allen, and Gatell, Frank Otto, eds. *The Segregation Era 1863–1954.* New York: Oxford, 1970.

Wharton, Vernon Lane. *The Negro in Mississippi, 1865–1890.* New York: Harper, 1965.

Wiedner, Donald L. *A History of Africa.* New York: Vintage, 1964.

Wiley, Bell Irvin. *Southern Negroes, 1861–1865.* New Haven: Yale University Press, 1965.

Williams, Eric. *Capitalism and Slavery.* New York: Capricorn, 1966.

Williamson, Joel. *After Slavery: The Negro in South Carolina During Reconstruction, 1861–1877.* Chapel Hill: University of North Carolina Press, 1965.

Wish, Harvey, ed. *Reconstruction in the South, 1865–1877.* New York: Farrar Straus & Giroux, 1965.

Woodward, C. Vann. *Origins of the New South, 1877–1913.* Baton Rouge: Louisiana State University Press, 1966.

Woodward, C. Vann. *Reunion and Reaction: The Compromise of 1877 and the End of Reconstruction.* New York: Little Brown, 1966.

Woodward, C. Vann. *The Strange Career of Jim Crow.* New York: Oxford, 1966.

Zilversmit, Arthur. *The First Emancipation: The Abolition of Slavery in the North*. Chicago: University of Chicago Press, 1967.

Zinn, Howard. *SNCC: The New Abolitionists*. Boston: Beacon, 1964.

Index

Index

250

Index

Index

Index